OXFORD WORLD'S CLASSICS

IDYLLS

THEOCRITUS was a native of Syracuse in Sicily; he was probably born in the last two years of the fourth century BC. Very little is known of the details of his life, but the subjects of his poetry cover Sicily and the Greek west, the eastern Aegean (notably the island of Cos), and Alexandria, the capital of the Ptolemaic empire. He appears to have sought or enjoyed the patronage of Hieron II of Syracuse and Ptolemy II Philadelphus, who reigned at Alexandria between 283 and 246 BC, and internal indications suggest links with Callimachus and Apollonius of Rhodes, the greatest poetic figures of Philadelphus' court. Theocritus' innovative 'bucolic' poems, vignettes of country life centred on competitions in song and love, are the foundational poems of the western pastoral tradition. The great variety of his other poems—hymns, short narrative epics, mimes, epigrams—illustrate the rich and flourishing poetic culture of what was a golden age for Greek poetry.

ANTHONY VERITY was formerly Headmaster of Leeds Grammar School and Master of Dulwich College. In his retirement he acts as an educational consultant.

RICHARD HUNTER is Regius Professor of Greek, University of Cambridge.

D0167681

OXFORD WORLD'S CLASSICS

——

THEOCRITUS

Idylls

——

Translated by
ANTHONY VERITY

With an Introduction and Notes by
RICHARD HUNTER

OXFORD
UNIVERSITY PRESS

OXFORD

UNIVERSITY PRESS

Great Clarendon Street, Oxford OX2 6DP

Oxford University Press is a department of the University of Oxford.
It furthers the University's objective of excellence in research, scholarship,
and education by publishing worldwide in

Oxford New York

Auckland Bangkok Buenos Aires Cape Town Chennai
Dar es Salaam Delhi Hong Kong Istanbul Karachi Kolkata
Kuala Lumpur Madrid Melbourne Mexico City Mumbai Nairobi
São Paulo Shanghai Taipei Tokyo Toronto

Oxford is a registered trade mark of Oxford University Press
in the UK and in certain other countries

Published in the United States
by Oxford University Press Inc., New York

© Anthony Verity and Richard Hunter 2002

The moral rights of the author have been asserted

Database right Oxford University Press (maker)

First published 2002
First published as an Oxford World's Classics paperback 2003

British Library Cataloguing in Publication Data

Data available

Library of Congress Cataloging in Publication Data

Theocritus.
[Idylls. English]
[Idylls/Theocritus; translated by Anthony Verity; with introduction and explanatory
notes by Richard Hunter.
p. cm.—(Oxford world's classics).
Includes bibliographical references.
1. Pastoral poetry, Greek—Translations into English.   2. Mediterranean Region—Poetry.
3. Country life—Poetry.   I. Verity, Anthony.   II. Hunter, Richard.   III. Title.
PA4443.E5 V47 2002   884'.01—dc21   2002072788

ISBN 0-19-283984-5

1 3 5 7 9 10 8 6 4 2

Printed in Great Britain by
Clays Ltd., St Ives plc

Contents

Introduction

> Who would not sing for Lycidas? He knew
> Himself to sing, and build the lofty rhyme.
> He must not float upon his wat'ry bier
> Unwept, and welter to the parching wind,
> Without the meed of some melodious tear.

BEHIND Milton's verses lie centuries of pastoral verse, but their source is to be traced to the *Boukolika* ('ox-herding poems') of Theocritus of Syracuse (mid-third century BC) who bequeathed to the Western tradition the lament for the death of a pastoral poet (Idyll 1), the peculiar pathos of death by drowning (Idylls 1 and 13), and the very name 'Lycidas' (Idyll 7). Idylls 1, 3, 4–7, 10 and (to a lesser extent) 11 represent something quite new in Greek poetry.[1] Theocritus' extraordinarily influential invention assures him an honourable mention in most histories of Western literature, but the variety and breadth of his poetry is less often appreciated. Moreover, although he is rightly viewed as standing at the head of the pastoral tradition (often called 'Sicilian' or 'Syracusan' because of him, cf. Virgil, *Ecl.* 6. 1, 10. 51), his 'bucolic' poetry differed in many ways from what followed, and 'pastoral' really evolved from particular imitations and 'readings' of, first, Theocritus and, subsequently, of Theocritus' greatest imitator, Virgil.[2] As a literary elaboration of popular, non-literate song (cf. Section 3 below), Theocritus' poems may be better understood against the background of other analogous phenomena in Hellenistic poetry than through the tradition of later pastoral. Nevertheless, of all poetic genres, it is epic and its rustic cousin pastoral[3] which give the greatest prominence to the idea of 'succession' in poetry, that is of later poets as the heirs of their predecessors, and Theocritus'

---

[1] Idylls 8 and 9 are not by Theocritus, and have not been included in this book.

[2] Cf. below, p. xvii.

[3] For epic and pastoral cf. below, p. xvi.

herdsmen too carry with them this sense of the past and its loss, embodied in the story of the founding poet, Daphnis (Idyll 1). To this extent, Theocritus may indeed be properly viewed through the lens of what later centuries made of his creation.

I. THEOCRITUS[4]

Theocritus' poetic career probably began in the late 280s and extended into the middle of the third century BC; Idylls 14, 15, and 17 belong to the reign at Alexandria of Ptolemy Philadelphus (*c*.283–246) and the latter two poems to the period of Philadelphus' marriage to Arsinoe (*c*.276–270 or 268). He came from Sicily, very probably from Syracuse itself, and the identifiable settings for his poems are Sicily and South Italy (?1, 4, 5, 6), Cos (7), and Alexandria (15). Many indications point to a context within the flourishing intellectual and poetic culture of the Eastern Aegean in the early Hellenistic period: Theocritus' friendship with the doctor and poet Nicias of Miletus (Idylls 11, 13, 28) and the allusions in Idyll 7 by 'Simichidas' to Asclepiades of Samos and Philitas of Cos place Theocritus at the heart of a remarkable period for Greek poetry (cf. below). It has, moreover, been shown that the flora of the bucolic poems belongs very largely to Greece and the Aegean, not to Sicily, even when the poems are set in the West;[5] we cannot, therefore, assume that an 'early' Sicilian period was followed by a later career in the east, particularly in the cities within the Ptolemaic orbit. Rather, Theocritus may fit the model of a 'professional poet', not tied to the traditions and performance contexts of a single city, but travelling freely to the various centres of Greek culture and with ties of friendship and patronage throughout the Mediterranean; this is a world of which we catch glimpses in the poetry of Callimachus and which Theocritus himself appears to depict, with a satiric edge, in the portrait of 'Simichidas' in Idyll 7.

---

[4] Some material in this Introduction is re-used from the Introduction to Hunter, *Theocritus: A Selection*. Where full bibliographical information is not given, it will be found in the 'Select Bibliography'.

[5] A. Lindsell, 'Was Theocritus a botanist?', *Greece & Rome*, 6 (1937), 78–93, reprinted in J. E. Raven, *Plants and Plant Lore in Ancient Greece* (Oxford, 2000), 65–75.

Despite this apparent mobility within the Aegean world, Idylls 14, 15, 17, and the lost poem *Berenice* take us explicitly to the Alexandria of Ptolemy Philadelphus; there is an all but certain reference to this king in Idyll 7, set on Cos, which enjoyed Philadelphus' protection, and Ptolemaic contexts have plausibly been argued also for Idylls 18 and 24. It therefore seems very likely that Theocritus worked extensively within the sphere of Ptolemaic patronage, at least during the 270s.[6] Moreover, very clear textual links between certain poems of Theocritus and the poetry of Callimachus and Apollonius of Rhodes, who both worked as scholar-poets in mid-third-century Alexandria,[7] may plausibly be traced to Alexandria, or at least to a shared poetic context.[8]

Of the thirty poems (or Idylls)[9] collected in standard editions of Theocritus some twenty-two are generally accepted as the work of Theocritus himself (and it is these which are presented here in Anthony Verity's new translation). We also have a fragment of a lost poem entitled *Berenice* (presumably in honour of the mother of Philadelphus and Arsinoe), and signs of another lost paederastic poem ('Idyll 31'); there are also twenty-five epigrams ascribed to Theocritus, though in some cases the ascription must be regarded as doubtful.[10] The poems were presumably first recited and/or circulated by Theocritus separately; some may have been collected together and 'published' shortly after Theocritus' death, or even by Theocritus himself, but the first collection of which anything is known was by Artemidorus of Tarsus in the first half of the first century BC. This collection seems to be memorialized in a well-known epigram by Artemidorus: 'The bucolic Muses were once scattered, but now they are all together in one pen and one

---

[6] Cf. Griffiths, *Theocritus at Court*; Hunter, *Theocritus: Encomium of Ptolemy*.

[7] Idyll 17 is clearly related to Callimachus' hymns to Zeus and Delos, and Idylls 13 (*Hylas*) and 22 (*The Dioscuri*) are very closely related to two corresponding episodes on either side of the division between Books 1 and 2 of Apollonius' *Argonautica*.

[8] There is, however, no evidence that Theocritus also wrote scholarly prose works, as did Callimachus and Apollonius, and relatively little sign (again compared to the other two great names) in the poems themselves of an engagement with the philological and scholarly interpretation of (as distinct from imitation and verbal variation of) Homer.

[9] The origin of the term *eidullia*, which the scholia apply to all of Theocritus' poems (not just 'the bucolics') is unclear; 'little types' is a plausible book title, particularly given the variety of Theocritus' poetry, but no date can firmly be attached to it.

[10] Cf. L. Rossi, *The Epigrams ascribed to Theocritus: A Method of Approach* (Leuven 2001).

herd' (*Anthologia Palatina* 9. 205). This may well have been the collection in which Virgil read Theocritus.

2. THEOCRITUS AND POST-CLASSICAL POETRY

If our view of the later fifth century is dominated by the drama of classical Athens, the fourth century seems by contrast the age of (again largely Athenian) philosophy and rhetoric. Little poetry survives from this period, other than the comedies of Menander from the very end of the century. Nevertheless, we know the names of many poets and can identify certain trends, particularly in comedy and dithyramb; moreover, hindsight allows us to discern patterns amidst the fragments, which assume significance in the light of what was to come. One of these is indeed the gradual re-emergence of other cultural centres from out of the shadow cast by Athens, both in the west and in the eastern Aegean; the poetry of Theocritus will suggest a whole world of poetic and personal relations stretching from Syracuse to the coast of Asia Minor.

The principal figures of archaic and classical poetry were specialists in both words and music, but the great age of lyric and choral poetry seems to have been over by the end of the fifth century, and an increasing separation of the purely textual from the more broadly 'performative' aspects of poetry is reflected in the fact that most poetry is now written in hexameters or elegiacs, the two most versatile, 'all-purpose' of Greek metres. Poets remained, of course, free to experiment—as witness Theocritus' 'Aeolic' poems, Idylls 28–30 (cf. below)—but such experiments were often enough, as with Theocritus, virtuoso reconstructions of now defunct forms. Public 'performance' remained very important, but this performance now increasingly took the form of recitation which was not musically accompanied. By an apparent paradox, we may be reminded of the situation of the archaic age in which rhapsodes performed epic song at the courts of great men (as famously exemplified by Demodocus at the court of Alcinous in the *Odyssey*) or at religious festivals, such as the Delian festival for Apollo described in the *Homeric Hymn to Apollo*. This situation had in essence never changed, though our evidence for it is swamped by the prominence of Athenian public drama. So too, the sophisticated cultural milieu of the Hellenistic courts at Alexandria, Pella, Antioch and elsewhere continues the practice of great figures of earlier ages, such as Polycrates of Samos, Hieron I of Syracuse, and Archelaos of Macedon, whose riches attracted poets, philosophers, and scientists to take up residence at their courts.

Changes in Greek poetry during this period can only be understood against the background of increased written circulation of texts and the gradual creation of an 'international' reading audience, which, though relatively very small, came to form an increasingly important élite. To what extent poetry, as well as culture more generally, gradually divides into the 'élite' and the 'popular' after the fifth century is a matter of much dispute, but it is clear that the very exercise of reading 'literature' could act as a powerful tool of selection. Attic drama was performed and re-performed before very large audiences throughout the Greek world, but by the end of the fifth century only a very tiny minority, represented comically by the aesthete Dionysus in Aristophanes' *Frogs*, would read texts of plays as well as watch them (*Frogs* 52–3). Such a development clearly goes hand-in-hand with the simplification of Greek metrics and the fact that major poets no longer wrote choral lyric, but it is also tempting to seek other changes in poetic style which go along with the increased exploitation of literacy. In particular, a marked density of intertextual allusion, the literary process by which meaning is created through various forms of allusion to other texts, is normally thought only possible in a written literature. Epic songs may refer to each other or to the epic tradition in general, just as the *Odyssey* seems clearly to exploit our knowledge of martial epic, if not of the *Iliad* in particular, the lyric and elegiac poets of the archaic age exploit their audience's knowledge of particular epic scenes and motifs, Attic comedies of the fifth century not merely thrive on tragic parody but also allude to each other almost obsessively, and there is very likely much more allusion (both textual and performative) from one tragedy to another than we can now reconstruct; nevertheless, forms of allusion which depend upon close verbal reference to small passages of earlier texts intensify with the spread of reading as a principal mode of reception. This is most obvious, of course, in texts which have a single principal model to which readers are constantly referred: Virgil's use of Theocritus in the *Eclogues* and Apollonius' use of Homer are obvious examples.

There is no single Theocritean mode of allusiveness. In Idyll 2, Simaetha's account of Delphis' visit assimilates him by textual allusion to the Homeric Odysseus, particularly in the latter's encounter with the Phaeacian princess Nausicaa, one of several rôle-models from high literature after which Simaetha fashions her 'grand passion' with the young man who has now abandoned her; her elaborate reworking in vv. 106–10 of Sappho's famous description (fr. 31) of the physical symptoms of desire is a further example of how she authorizes her experience through the great texts of the past. The clearest Theocritean example of the extended use of a single model is the use of *Odyssey* 9, the story of Odysseus and the Cyclops, in Idyll 11, the song of the lovesick Cyclops. The comic pathos of the song derives not merely from the very idea that the cannibal monster of the *Odyssey* could be a tender and lovesick young man, and one whose experience could serve as a paradigm for all of humanity, but also from the dramatic irony by which our knowledge of the future allows us to read more into the Cyclops' words than he himself intends. Other extended examples of Theocritean allusiveness are the birth of Philadelphus in Idyll 17, which rewrites the birth of Apollo in the *Homeric Hymn to Apollo*, and the extensive use of Euripides' *Bacchae* in Idyll 26, which tells the story of Pentheus' horrible end. A poem with a particularly 'thick' allusive texture is Idyll 24, which makes detailed use of two Pindaric versions of the story of Heracles and the snakes (cf. Section 4 below), as well as epic poems which tell of mysterious nocturnal events (*Odyssey* 20, *Homeric Hymn to Demeter*). Idyll 16, in honour of Hieron of Syracuse, contains many echoes of the encomiastic poetry of an earlier age, particularly that of Pindar and Simonides. The relationship between the narratives of Hylas (Id. 13) and Amycus (Id. 22) and the parallel accounts in Apollonius' *Argonautica* form a special case of close intertextual play between contemporary poets.

Beyond these particular reworkings, we are reminded of earlier literature at every turn, whether of specific scenes which have survived—the marvellous cup of Idyll 1 is clearly a latter-day version of the Shield of Achilles from *Iliad* 1, the encounter with the mysterious Lycidas in Idyll 7 replays Hesiod's meeting with the Muses at the start of the *Theogony*—or of more general situations, such as of Spartan maiden-songs in Idyll 18 and of more serious 'lover's serenades' in Idyll 3, the song of a deluded goatherd outside his beloved's cave. The allusive texture is not, of course, uniformly thick. Idylls 4 and 5 offer representations of different types of rustic 'exchange' which look to poetic traditions which had not previously entered into high literature (cf. below, Section 3).

3. BUCOLIC POETRY

The earliest collections of Theocritus' poetry of which we know were called *Boukolika*, and this is the title which Virgil too adopted for his 'pastoral' poems; Idyll 1, which headed all ancient collections, has the refrain 'Begin, my Muses, begin the herdsman's song (*boukolikas . . . aoidas*)', and it is clear that Theocritus himself uses the description 'bucolic' as a significant marker of his own poetry. What, however, did he mean by it? 'Bucolic' terminology in Theocritus seems in fact to suggest the exchange of song, usually within the framework of a 'song contest';[11] with the exception of the legendary Daphnis 'the oxherd' himself (Id. 1, perhaps also 6) and Damoetas (Id. 6), Theocritus' musical herdsmen are not oxherds (*boukoloi*), and it is unlikely that 'bucolic song' simply commemorates the tragic figure of Idyll 1. Theocritus perhaps wants his audience to think of (real or believed) traditions of Sicilian 'bucolic' song-making of which we catch a glimpse in a notice in Athenaeus (14. 619a–b): 'There was a song for people leading flocks, the so-called *boukoliasmos*. Diomos was a Sicilian oxherd, and he invented this type; Epicharmus mentions him in the *Alkyon* and the *Shipwrecked Odysseus*.' Epicharmus wrote comedies at Syracuse in the first half of the fifth century and was for Theocritus a major figure of the Sicilian literary past; part at least of the explanation for the Doric colouring of the bucolic poems must be to signal an affiliation to the traditions of western

---

[11] Cf. Hunter, *Theocritus: A Selection*, 5–9.

Greece. Whatever lies behind this notice in Athenaeus, it seems clear that the existence of 'bucolic' poetry at Syracuse was in fact widely accepted from an early date: the lyric poet Philoxenus seems to have exploited these Sicilian traditions for his famous *Cyclops or Galatea* of the early fourth century (imitated by Theocritus in Id. 11),[12] and Euripides' *Cyclops*, set on Sicily, contains a very 'Theocritean' song (41–62), which may, like the Theocritean Cyclops of Idylls 6 and 11, similarly exploit the audience's belief in such a Sicilian tradition. Real shepherds and goatherds did no doubt, then as now, fill the long watching hours with music and song, including competitions of various levels of formality, and this had always been part of how such 'simple people' were imagined in art: already in the *Iliad* Hephaestus depicts on the Shield of Achilles 'two herdsmen amusing themselves with the syrinx' unaware of the treachery which awaited (18. 525–6). A naive and unworldly trustingness was to remain an integral part of the characters of pastoral literature throughout the western tradition; when events from the world of politics and war impinge upon them, as in Virgil's *Eclogues*, they are reflected through the simplicity of this (often uncomprehending) vision.

Hellenistic art and literature seem to show a greater interest in the countryside and its people than is obvious earlier. The epigrams of Anyte of Arcadian Tegea present dedications to Pan and the nymphs and inscriptions which invite weary travellers to rest and cool themselves, and the epigrams of Leonidas of Tarentum, roughly contemporary with Theocritus, offer a whole series of rustic dedications, including one to Hermes and Pan in a rural spot of stylized beauty (what become known as a *locus amoenus*). These movements in Hellenistic culture are often associated by modern critics with the increasing urbanization of life and a nostalgic longing for simplicity, as 'Simichidas' must go 'away from the town' at the opening of Idyll 7, but they cannot be considered in isolation from other artistic, intellectual, and social developments: Epicureanism, with its goal of *ataraxia* 'freedom from disturbance', Cynicism which preached a particularly hard brand of 'simplicity', and the 'realism' of Hellenistic art all suggest that no single explanation for this turn towards 'the simple life'

[12] Cf. Aristophanes, *Plutus* 290–315.

will be adequate; for Theocritus, as we have seen, there is also the importance of the performative traditions of Western Greece. As for the descriptions of the countryside themselves, it is important that such poetic descriptions are, to some extent, inevitably repetitive—particularly in a hot climate such as that of Greece, where the presence of water and shade is always likely to be important, and where, moreover, a detailed particularity in the landscape is only rarely the focus of poetic interest; thus the description of a 'real' landscape, i.e. one with which the poet and/or the audience is familiar and to which geographically specific names may be attached, may be barely distinguishable from an 'imaginary' landscape, which in any case will be built by the imagination from both visual and intellectual experience. So too, the use of or allusion to the landscape descriptions of Homer are as common in 'real' as in 'imaginary' settings; ancient poets habitually see through the lenses of prior texts. Within this general framework, it is to be noted that modern experts credit Theocritus with some botanical knowledge and an ability to describe flowers evocatively, to place them in their correct contexts and environments and to distinguish between them to a very unusual degree (for Greek poetry).[13] Whether this knowledge derives in large part from books (? Theophrastus) or from personal observation may be disputed, but elsewhere too Hellenistic poets are concerned to reproduce 'scientific' phenomena as accurately as poetry allows, and Theocritean 'realism' must be viewed in this wider context.

Greek literature did not, of course, suddenly discover the countryside in the Hellenistic period. Of particular importance for Theocritus is Plato's *Phaedrus*, in which the very urban Socrates, for once out of his 'natural habitat', specifically draws attention to the beauties of nature—cool water, the shade of a plane-tree, statues of the Nymphs, cicada song—and marks them as aesthetic pleasures inimical to intellectual progress (230b–d). The *Phaedrus* establishes 'the countryside' as the appropriate place for the exchange of performances about love. Socrates tells a myth of the origin of cicadas from men who were so besotted with the new pleasure of song that they neglected to eat and drink (258e6–9d8); for Socrates, the highest form of 'worship of the Muses' is

---

[13] Cf. Lindsell and Raven cited in n. 2 above.

philosophy, but in the world of Theocritean bucolic, song is more often than not the result of emotional distress, for it is the eruption of desire into the bucolic world which destroys the hoped-for *hasychia* ('quietness') and shatters the 'idyllic' world of an Anyte. Song is both a product of desire and may bring temporary alleviation from it (10. 21–3, Id. 11), but it really only serves to highlight human distress, a distress not felt by the animals that the herdsmen guard (1. 151–2, 3. 2–5, etc.). The 'sufferings of Daphnis', who apparently rejected desire and died for it, is the founding myth of bucolic poetry: all Theocritus' bucolic characters seek to match Daphnis' 'heroism', and all fall short, because such rejection can indeed only exist in the thought-experiment world of myth.

The world of the bucolic poems is, from one perspective, the world which epic forgot. The description of the marvellous cup in Idyll 1 depicting different types and stages of life asserts a parallelism and opposition to the scenes on the shield of Achilles in *Iliad* 18, scenes which were taken to represent the rich variety of the cosmos: where the Iliadic scenes are introduced and framed by the constellations which very visibly surround us all (*Iliad* 18. 485–9), the Theocritean scenes are set within a delicate ivy pattern which calls attention to itself only on the closest inspection. So too, whereas the shield of Achilles, on which 'syrinx-playing' herdsmen are merely a small detail, is forged in Hephaestus' marvellous workshop with its vast array of bellows, costly metals, and 'huge anvil', the bowl of Idyll 1 is itself the creation of a syrinx-playing goatherd and was obtained from an entirely obscure ferryman on an obscure island for the price of a goat and a cheese. This tension between, on the one hand, the self-conscious humbleness of the characters and their world, a world hidden from our view and indeed, unlike the world of epic, almost from our imagination, and, on the other, the literary and intellectual pretension of the hexameters, the metre of Homer, in which these characters express themselves, is naturally productive of various ironic effects, but Theocritus certainly does not sneer at his rustics. Gentle mockery is reserved in fact for Simichidas, the young and over-confident poet of the extraordinary Idyll 7, the *Thalysia* ('harvest festival'). In this reflection upon the creation of an artificial poetic world, the narrator, Simichidas, tells of a trip into the Coan countryside where he met Lycidas, who 'looked very like a goatherd', but whose appearance and behaviour strongly suggests divinity (? Apollo). The two exchange songs (*boukoliazesthai*) on erotic themes, and Lycidas gives Simichidas his staff, in a rewriting of Hesiod's initiation by the Muses at the opening of the *Theogony*. The poem dramatizes the ironic truth, one not yet fully appreciated by Simichidas, that the relation between the 'real' countryside and the literary construction which is 'bucolic' poetry is complex and shifting, and cannot be reduced to a universal metaphoric code.

Although none of the bucolic poems is quite like any other, the impression is of the constant rearrangement and fresh patterning of elements drawn from a repertoire which seems familiar, but is in fact being newly created before our eyes. Most remarkably, perhaps, no single structural pattern is repeated in any of the exchanges or contests of songs (Idylls 1, 4–7, 10). Constant difference within the apparently unchanging and familiar was indeed to remain a feature of the bucolic/pastoral tradition, and it already marks the world which Theocritus creates. That world is, however, not (yet) the world of later European pastoral. After Theocritus 'bucolic' turned into 'pastoral' by a concentration upon certain aspects of Theocritus' poems, notably love and the relations between man and nature and between present and mythical past, to the exclusion of others, and gradually gave greater prominence to the metaphor of the poet as herdsman. The irony with which Idylls 7, 10, and 11, at least, self-consciously exploit their scripted rusticity slowly gave way to a 'pastoral' code shared by poet, characters, and audience, which often strikes modern readers as 'sentimental' in comparison with Theocritus' hard edge; thus, for example, Theocritus associates the 'pathetic fallacy' with the mythical death of Daphnis, whereas later pastoral freely extends this trope into the contemporary world of the characters. Theocritus' compositions should be seen also within the context of third-century experimentation with new poetic modes and an interest in the lives of 'ordinary' people; his rustics are indeed rustics and 'herding' is not (merely) a stylized way of describing poetic composition. Later pastoral (broadly speaking) accepts 'rusticity' as a conventional poetic mode, and one in which allegory flourished, as indeed allegorical interpretation set in early in the history of the reception of Virgil's *Eclogues*. It is noteworthy that it is the young poet 'Simichidas' in Idyll 7 who shows the way to the future both because he indeed treats 'rusticity' as a conventional code, and because he is the Theocritean character who gave the strongest impulse toward allegorical interpretation; that 'Simichidas' *is* Theocritus was the almost unanimous assumption of ancient commentators upon the poem.[14]

Idylls 1 and 3–7 are distinguished rhythmically in their hexameters from Theocritus' other poems, and it is not unreasonable to think that he saw them as a distinct sub-group within his oeuvre. They are also characterized by symmetries of language, structure, and thought which suggest, rather than conceal, the artificiality of the 'natural' world which they depict. This mannerism of style, perhaps nowhere more obvious than in the opening of the 'programmatic' Idyll 1 in which order and hierarchy are at issue in the subject as well as the style of the verses, was to remain with pastoral literature throughout its long history, and indeed came to be exaggerated far beyond Theocritean practice, as in Longus' *Daphnis and Chloe*. Here too the subsequent tradition filled out gestures of the Theocritean text into full-blown generic markers.

4. THE NON-BUCOLIC POEMS

The Theocritean corpus offers the best view available to us of the rich variety of Hellenistic poetic forms. Moreover, though many different sub-groupings of these poems are possible, the collection as a whole is resistant to scholastic and formalist approaches to 'genre': apparently 'bucolic' elements appear in the poems for Hieron and Ptolemy (Idylls 16 and 17) and the hymn to the Dioscuri (Idyll 22), and Idyll 11, the song of the lovesick Cyclops, has important links both with the mythological narrative of Idyll 13 (Heracles and Hylas) and with the performance of the spurned goatherd (Idyll 3). So too, some poems are wholly 'mimetic' or dramatic in shape (Idylls 1, 2, 3–5, 10, 14–15), i.e. without any

---

[14] For an exception cf. scholium (a) on 7. 21.

explanatory introduction, whereas in others mimetic elements are surrounded or introduced by an authorial frame (Idylls 6, 11) or even startlingly introduced in the middle of hymnic narrative (Idyll 22).

Real or believed traditions of rustic, folkloric song by no means exhaust Theocritus' debt to the cultural heritage of his native Syracuse. The preserved ancient commentaries allege some influence in Idylls 2 and 15 from the 'mimes' of Sophron of Syracuse (fifth century). The scope and length of Sophron's mimes is uncertain, but it is probably not unfair to think of them as playlets, written, at least in part, in a kind of rhythmical prose. They seem to have been divided into those with male and those with female characters, and it is noteworthy that among the former were 'The Fisherman and the Countryman' and 'The Tunny-Fisherman'. Sophron enjoyed a particular reputation for the depiction of character (*ēthopoiia*), and Simaetha of Idyll 2 and Gorgo and Praxinoa in Idyll 15 indeed remain among the most memorable 'characters' of Greek literature. Gorgo and Praxinoa are (? like Theocritus) Syracusans living in Alexandria, and their 'day off' at the royal palace dramatizes the coming of Syracusan mime traditions—and the poet of those traditions, Theocritus himself—to the new cultural centre of the Greek world. Moreover, the opening exchanges of Idyll 15, with their frequent change of speaker in mid-verse, come perhaps as close as is possible to depriving the hexameter of its poetic quality. Theocritus thus takes an elevated verse form and dismantles it in the direction of prose; such mimes may thus be seen as productive transgressions of received ideas of a fitting linkage between metrical and verbal style, on one hand, and subject-matter on the other.

Another traditional poetic form which is very influential in the Theocritean corpus is the hymn, and particularly the hexametric *Homeric Hymns*: the encomium of Philadelphus (Idyll 17), the hymns to the Dioscuri (Idyll 22) and to Dionysus (Idyll 26), and the narrative of the infant Heracles (Idyll 24) may all be considered as (at least in part) modern versions of this genre. The 'Hymn to the Dioscuri' shows particularly well Theocritus' consciousness of the history of the form, as it begins with a close reworking of the 'Homeric Hymn to the Dioscuri' and then follows this with juxtaposed 'hymns' of very varying styles to the individual brothers; it is almost as though Theocritus is here exploring the range of possibilities open to him. Political realignments in the Hellenistic world, which gave a new importance to powerful individuals and rulers, also gave new life to the language of encomium, and it is here that the hymn comes into its own. Idyll 24 also illustrates Theocritus' engagement with the lyric tradition, as the story of Heracles and the snakes had been handled twice by Pindar (*Nemean* 1, *Paean* 20); the humorous account of the homelife of Heracles' parents—Alcmena rocks her children to sleep in a shield and sings them a lullaby—is, however, a long way from Pindar's heroic action. Choral lyric also lies behind Idyll 18, a recreation of the epithalamium sung by Helen's girlfriends on the night of her wedding to Menelaus, a poem which evokes the beautiful but lost world of Spartan culture (cf. Alcman's 'Partheneion'), and is also very important in Idyll 16, the encomium and request for patronage to Hieron II, an extraordinary blend of hymn, mime, and popular begging-song; in this last poem many motifs from the victory-songs of Pindar and Simonides reveal Theocritus' creative awareness of the similarities and differences between modern poetic culture and that of the past. Idylls 28–30 reproduce the language and themes of the great lyric poets of Lesbos, Sappho and Alcaeus, but stichic metre (i.e. the constant repetition of the same verse form, as for example in Homer) rather than the stanzaic arrangement of the 'originals' is an accommodation to an age which had lost touch with archaic and classical musical forms and in which recitation and reading were the two principal modes of reception.

Select Bibliography

For fuller information cf. A. Köhnken and R. Kirstein, 'Theokrit 1950–1994 (1996)', *Lustrum*, 37 (1995) 203–307, and the bibliography in R. Hunter, *Theocritus: A Selection* (below).

Editions and Commentaries

The standard modern Greek text (with translation) and commentary is A. S. F. Gow, *Theocritus*, 2nd edn. (Cambridge, 1952). Smaller-scale commentaries are K. J. Dover, *Theocritus: Select Poems* (London, 1971; contains *Idylls* 1–7, 10, 11, 13–16, 18, 22, 24, 26, 28), and R. Hunter, *Theocritus: A Selection* (Cambridge, 1999; contains *Idylls* 1, 3, 4, 6, 7, 10, 11, 13). Among studies of individual poems cf. A. Sens, *Theocritus: Dioscuri (Idyll 22)* (Göttingen, 1997), and R. Hunter, *Theocritus: Encomium of Ptolemy* (below).

Hellenistic Poetry

P. Bing, *The Well-Read Muse: Present and Past in Callimachus and the Hellenistic Poets* (Göttingen, 1988).

A. W. Bulloch, 'Hellenistic Poetry', in P. E. Easterling and B. M. W. Knox (eds.), *The Cambridge History of Classical Literature*, i. *Greek Literature* (Cambridge, 1985), 541–621.

P. M. Fraser, *Ptolemaic Alexandria* (Oxford, 1972).

S. Goldhill, *The Poet's Voice* (Cambridge, 1991).

G. Hutchinson, *Hellenistic Poetry* (Oxford, 1988).

G. Zanker, *Realism in Alexandrian Poetry: a Literature and its Audience* (London, 1987).

Theocritus and Later Pastoral

P. Alpers, *What is Pastoral?* (Chicago, 1996).

T. Hubbard, *The Pipes of Pan* (Ann Arbor, 1998).

T. G. Rosenmeyer, *The Green Cabinet: Theocritus and the European Pastoral Lyric* (Berkeley, 1969).

The Bucolic Poems

K. J. Gutzwiller, *Theocritus' Pastoral Analogies: The Formation of a Genre* (Madison, Wis., 1991).

D. M. Halperin, *Before Pastoral: Theocritus and the Ancient Tradition of Bucolic Poetry* (New Haven/London, 1983).

G. Lawall, *Theocritus' Coan Pastorals* (Washington, DC, 1967).

C. P. Segal, *Poetry and Myth in Ancient Pastoral* (Princeton, 1981).

The Non-Bucolic Poems

J. B. Burton, *Theocritus' Urban Mimes: Mobility, Gender, and Patronage* (Berkeley, 1995).

F. T. Griffiths, *Theocritus at Court* (Leiden, 1979).

R. Hunter, *Theocritus and the Archaeology of Greek Poetry* (Cambridge, 1996).

R. Hunter, *Theocritus: Encomium of Ptolemy* (Berkeley/Los Angeles, forthcoming).

Further Reading in Oxford World's Classics

The Homeric Hymns, trans. and ed. Michael Crudden.

Apollonius of Rhodes, *Jason and the Golden Fleece*, trans. and ed. Richard Hunter.

Longus, *Daphnis and Chloe*, trans. and ed. Ronald McCail.

Plato, *Phaedrus*, trans. and ed. Robin Waterfield.

Virgil, *The Eclogues and The Georgics*, trans. C. Day Lewis, ed. R. O. A. M. Lyne.

Note on the Translation

This translation is from the Oxford Classical Text of A. S. F. Gow, with a few minor variations. Marginal line numbers refer to the Greek text.

I have tried as far as possible to match Theocritus line for line, but have not hesitated to expand or contract the English version where this makes the meaning clearer. Bold departures from the Greek, usually in the case of proverbial or idiomatic expressions, are explained in the notes.

I have used Latinized spellings of Greek names, except in a few cases where this would look especially odd.

Theocritus presents the translator with some tricky problems, most noticeably in his frequent shifts of register. In this connection I have benefited greatly from the criticism and encouragement of Professors Richard Hunter and David West, and of Peter Jones, James Morwood, and Jan Piggott. Any inaccuracies or infelicities which remain are entirely my responsibility.

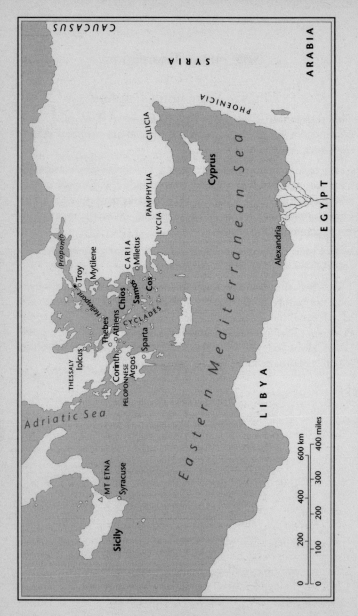

MAP: Theocritus' World. Acknowledgement: Andrew Morley

Idyll 1
Thyrsis' Lament for Daphnis

THYRSIS There is sweet music in that pine tree's whisper, goatherd,
  There by the spring. Sweet too is the music of your pipe;*
  You would win the second prize to Pan.* If he takes as his
  Reward a horned goat, you will have the she-goat. If he
  Wins the she-goat as a prize, the kid will fall to you.
  A kid's meat is good, until the time it gives its milk.
GOATHERD Shepherd, your song sounds sweeter than the water tumbling
  Over there from the high rock. If the Muses take a ewe
  As their prize, yours will be a stall-fed lamb. If they desire
  To take the lamb, then you will carry off the ewe.   10
THYRSIS Come and sit here, goatherd, please, for the Nymphs' sake,
  Where tamarisks grow and the land slopes away from this mound,
  And play your pipe; I shall pasture your goats meanwhile.
GOATHERD We're not allowed to pipe at midday, shepherd—not allowed.
  It's then that Pan rests, you know, tired from the hunt.
  We're afraid of him; he's tetchy at this hour, and his lip
  Is always curled in sour displeasure. But look, Thyrsis, you
  Have sung of *The Sufferings of Daphnis*,* and you outstrip
  All others in herdsman's song; so come, let's sit   20
  Here under this elm, facing Priapus'* image and the spring
  There by the oaks and that shepherds' seat. If you sing
  As once you did in the match with Libyan Chromis
  I'll give you three milkings of a goat that suckles twins,
  Yet has enough left to fill two pails. I'll give you too
  A deep cup,* sealed with a layer of sweet wax,

FIGURE: Cup in *Idyll* I. Acknowledgement: researched and drawn by Andrew Morley

Two-handled, newly made, still smelling of the knife.
At its lip winds an ivy pattern, ivy dotted with
Golden clusters; its tendrils twist this way and that,   30
Glorying in their yellow fruit. Inside the plant's frame is carved
(Truly gods' craft) a woman resplendent in a dress and circlet.
She stands between two men with fine long hair, who compete
In alternating song, but do not touch her heart. She smiles,
Glances at one, then turns to look at the other, while they,
Their eyes long swollen with love, keep on their useless toil.
Next to them is carved an old fisherman, who stands
On a jagged rock. Urgently he gathers up his great net   40
For the cast, the image of a man straining his back to a task.
You'd think he was at his strength's limit, so do the sinews
Swell all around his neck as he fishes. Grey-haired
He may be, but his strength is the strength of youth.
Not far from this sea-beaten old man there is a vineyard,
Heavily laden with dark ripe grape-clusters. A little boy
Watches over it, perched on a drystone wall.
Two foxes lurk nearby; one prowls down the vine rows,
Stealing the ripe fruit, while the other pits all her cunning
Against the boy's satchel. No respite for him, she reckons,   50
Till he has nothing left for breakfast but dry bread.
But he is twisting a pretty cricket-cage of asphodel,
Plaiting it with rushes, with never a thought for satchel
And vines, absorbed as he is in his weaving task.
All round the cup's base spreads pliant acanthus, a wonder
For goatherds to see and a marvel to strike your heart.
For it I gave a sailor from Calydnos* a goat and a huge cheese
Of white milk; but it's still spotless, and has never touched
My lips. My friend, I would gladly give it you, for your   60
Enjoyment, if you would sing me that delightful song.
Please—I don't speak in mockery; everyone knows you cannot
Take your song to Hades, place of oblivion, and save it there.

THYRSIS

'Begin, my Muses, begin the herdsman's song.'*

I am Thyrsis from Etna,* Thyrsis whose voice is sweet.

Where were you, Nymphs, when Daphnis wasted away,
Where were you? In the lovely dales of Peneus, or of Pindus?*
You were surely not by Anapus'* broad stream, nor the peak
Of Etna, nor frequenting the sacred waters of Acis.*

Begin, my Muses, begin the herdsman's song.   70

At his death jackals howled, and wolves howled for him;*
Even the lion in the woods lamented his passing.

Begin, my Muses, begin the herdsman's song.

Many an ox mourned at his feet, and many a bull,
And many a heifer, too, and calf sang dirges for him.

Begin, my Muses, begin the herdsman's song.

First came Hermes* from the mountain and asked: "Daphnis,
Who is it that torments you? Who do you long for so much?"

Begin, my Muses, begin the herdsman's song.

Then cowmen, shepherds, and goatherds all came asking   80
What was the cause of his grief. Priapus came and asked:
"Poor Daphnis, why are you wasting away? Your girl
Is scouring everywhere, woodland and spring . . .

Begin, my Muses, begin the herdsman's song.

Seeking you. Love is surely cruel to you, helpless man;
Men used to call you a cowman, but now you are more like
The goatherd, who when he sees the she-goats being
Mounted weeps tears because he was not born a billy-goat.

Begin, my Muses, begin the herdsman's song.

And you, when you see how the girls laugh, weep   90
Because you are not able to join in their dance."
To this the cowherd answered nothing, but nursed
His bitter love, nursed it up to its appointed end.

Begin, my Muses, begin again the herdsman's song.

And Cypris* too came to see him, laughing with delight,
But laughing in secret, feigning a heavy heart. She said:

"Did you really boast that you could give Love a fall?
Is it not you yourself who are thrown by cruel Love?"

Begin, my Muses, begin again the herdsman's song.

Then Daphnis answered: "Hard Cypris, vengeful Cypris,   100
Cypris hated by mortals; so you really believe that
My last sun has set? I tell you, even from Hades
Daphnis will prove to be a source of painful grief to Love.

Begin, my Muses, begin again the herdsman's song.

Is it not said that the cowherd and Cypris . . . but away with you
To your Anchises*—go to Ida where oaks and galingale grow,
And the bees hum melodiously about their hives,

Begin, my Muses, begin again the herdsman's song.

And Adonis* too is in his prime, pasturing his sheep,
Killing hares, and hunting every kind of wild beast.   110

Begin, my Muses, begin again the herdsman's song.

Or go and confront Diomedes* and say: 'I've beaten
The cowherd Daphnis, so come on, now *you* fight with me.'

Begin, my Muses, begin again the herdsman's song.

Farewell you wolves and jackals, farewell you bears that lurk
In the mountains. No more will Daphnis the cowherd
Haunt your thickets, woods and groves. Farewell, Arethusa,*
And you streams whose bright waters pour down Thybris'*
     side.

Begin, my Muses, begin again the herdsman's song.

I am Daphnis, the one who herded his cows here,   120
And who watered here his bulls and calves.

Begin, my Muses, begin again the herdsman's song.

O Pan, Pan, if you are now on Lycaeus'* long ridge,
Or are ranging over mighty Maenalus,* come to Sicily's island.
Leave the peak of Helice* and the lofty tomb of Arcas,
Son of Lycaon,* a thing of admiration even to the gods.

Now end, my Muses, end the herdsman's song.

Come, lord, take this pipe, sweet-smelling from pressed wax
And rounded at its lip. See how Love now drags me off to
    Hades.   130

Now end, my Muses, end the herdsman's song.

Now, you thorns and brambles, bring forth violets, and
Let the lovely narcissus flower on the juniper. Let
All things run contrary, since Daphnis is near to death.
Let the pine tree sprout pears, let hounds be torn by stags,
Let nightingales cry out to owls at the day's dawn.

Now end, my Muses, end the herdsman's song."

So he sang, and ended. Aphrodite wished to raise him again
To life, but the thread which the Fates had given him had all
    run out.
Daphnis came to the river,* and the waters closed above the
    man   140
Whom the Muses loved, and whom the Nymphs did not reject.

Now end, my Muses, end the herdsman's song.'

Give me the cup now, and the goat too so that I can milk her,
And pour the Muses an offering. Farewell, my Muses,
Farewell. I shall sing to you again, a more melodious song.

GOATHERD Thyrsis, may your tuneful mouth be filled with honey
And honeycombs, and may you eat the sweet figs
Of Aegilus,* for you sing more sweetly than the cicada.
Look, my friend, here is the bowl; see how well it smells—
You could believe it had been washed in the Hours'* spring.
Come over here, Ivy. You milk her, Thyrsis. Stop frisking,   151
You nannies, or the billy-goat will be up and after you.

Idyll 2
The Sorceress

Where are my bay leaves?* Thestylis, fetch them.
Where are my love charms? Wind fine red wool
Around the cup, so that I may bind* my unkind love to me.
Eleven days now he has stayed away, the brute,
And does not even care if I am alive or dead—
Not even a knock at the door. How cruel he is!
Eros and Aphrodite have trapped his fickle heart
And carried it off to some new lover, of that I'm sure.
Tomorrow I shall go to Timagetus' wrestling school;
I'll find him and protest at the way he's treating me.
But now, I shall bind him with fire magic. Come, Moon,   10
Shine bright, for it is to you I'll chant my soft spells,
And to Hecate* below the earth; at her approach dogs
Shiver as she goes among the tombs and dark blood of the dead.
Hail to you, dread Hecate! Stay with me to the end,
And make these drugs as powerful as Circe's* were,
Or those Medea* devised, or Perimede* of the golden hair.

Magic wheel, draw my lover home to me.*

First, barley grains must smoulder on the fire. Go on,
Thestylis, throw them on! Idiot, is your mind wandering?
Or do you too think I'm ridiculous, you stupid girl?   20
Throw the grains, and say, 'These are Delphis' bones I throw'.

Magic wheel, draw my lover home to me.

As Delphis brought me pain, so in revenge at Delphis
I burn these bay leaves. As they crackle loudly in the fire,
And suddenly flare, leaving no ash behind for us to see,
So too may the flesh of Delphis shrivel in the flames.

Magic wheel, draw my lover home to me.

Now I shall burn the bran. O Artemis,* you can shatter
Even Hades' hard adamant, or any substance denser than that—
Thestylis, listen, the dogs are howling through the town: 30
The goddess is at the crossroads! Quick, beat the bronze gong!*

Magic wheel, draw my lover home to me.

Listen, the sea is hushed, and hushed too are the winds;
Only the pain within my breast cannot be hushed.
I am all aflame for the man who (the shame of it!)
Stole my virginity and my woman's good name.

Magic wheel, draw my lover home to me.

As with the help of the goddess I melt this wax,
So may Delphis of Myndus* melt with sudden love.
As Aphrodite helps me to spin this whirler* of bronze,   40
So may he come spinning to the door of my house.

Magic wheel, draw my lover home to me.

Three libations I make, lady, and I pray three times.
If it's a woman who lies with him, or if it's a man,
May he forget them utterly as once, on the island of Dia,*
Men say that Theseus* forgot fair-haired Ariadne.*

Magic wheel, draw my lover home to me.

The Arcadians have a herb, coltsfoot, which drives insane
All the swift mares and their foals on the mountains there.
So may I see Delphis, stung like them into madness,   50
Leave the sleek* wrestling school and come to my house.

Magic wheel, draw my lover home to me.

Here is the fringe which Delphis lost from his cloak;
I shred it now and hurl it on to the raging fire.
Cruel Love, why do you, like some leech from the marshes,
Cling to my body and suck out all of its dark blood?

Magic wheel, draw my lover home to me.

Tomorrow I'll grind up a lizard* to make him a poison drink.
But now, Thestylis, take these herbs and smear them

Secretly over his threshold while it is still night,   60
And whisper as you do: 'These are Delphis' bones I smear'.

Magic wheel, draw my lover home to me.

She has gone; how shall I weep for my passion, all alone?
Where shall I begin? Who was it brought me this pain?

One day my friend Anaxo, the daughter of Eubulus,
Served as a basket-bearer* in a parade to Artemis' grove.
Wild beasts accompanied with her, among them a lioness.

Learn, lady Moon, how my love came about.*

Theumaridas' Thracian nurse (she's passed on now)   70
Who lived next door, begged and implored me to go
And watch the parade, so all unsuspecting I joined her.
I was wearing a lovely long linen dress, and over it
I had a beautiful shawl which Clearista had lent me.

Learn, lady Moon, how my love came about.

When we were half way along the road, near Lycon's house,
I caught sight of Delphis and Eudamippus walking together;
Their beards were more golden than the helichryse, and their
Glistening breasts shone brighter even than the moon, for they
Had just come from refreshing exercise at the wrestling school. 80

Learn, lady Moon, how my love came about.

One look, and I was mad;* my helpless heart caught fire,
My beauty disappeared. As for the procession, it went
Clean out of my mind, and I don't know how I reached home.
Some parching fever shook me in its grip—
Ten days, ten nights, I could not leave my bed.

Learn, lady Moon, how my love came about.

Often my skin turned as yellow as Zantean dye,*
I started to lose my hair, there was nothing left of me but
Skin and bones. There wasn't a witch's house I didn't   90
Visit, and I pestered the homes of spell-chanting hags.
But I could find no relief, and time was flying by.

Learn, lady Moon, how my love came about.

So I told my slave-girl, told her the truth: 'Thestylis,
I beg you, find me some cure for this cruel disease;
This man from Myndus possesses my whole being.
He often goes to Timagetus' wrestling school, and
Likes to take his ease there. Go there and look for him.

Learn, lady Moon, how my love came about.

And when you are sure he's alone, silently sign to him,   100
And say: "Simaetha invites you". Then bring him here.'
That's what I said. So she went and brought him,
Delphis of the shining skin. As soon as I saw him
Stepping lightly across the threshold at my door . . .

Learn, lady Moon, how my love came about.

From head to foot I became colder than snow,*
And sweat like watery dew dripped from my brow.
I couldn't utter a sound, not so much as the whimper
That babies make, calling in sleep to their mothers.
My whole fair body went rigid, stiff as a doll's.   110

Learn, lady Moon, how my love came about.

When he saw me, he fixed his faithless eyes on the ground,*
Sat on the bed, and sitting uttered these words:
'Truly, Simaetha, I was on my way. Your summons
Outran my coming by only so much as I
Just now beat graceful Philinus* in the sprint.

Learn, lady Moon, how my love came about.

I would have come, by sweet Love I would have come,
Just as night fell, with two or three of my friends,
Bringing Dionysus' apples* in my tunic's fold,   120
And wearing Heracles' holy garland* on my head—
White poplar, wreathed about with purple ribbons.

Learn, lady Moon, how my love came about.

If you had let me in, well, that would have turned out well
(My friends all call me handsome and light-footed):

One kiss on your pretty mouth, and I'd have slept content.
But if you had tried to keep me out and barred the door,
I tell you, axes and torches would have been your next callers.

Learn, lady Moon, how my love came about.   129

But here I am. So first I must give thanks to Cypris,* and after
Her to you, my lady: you saved me from the flames, half-burnt
As I was, when you invited me to your house. Often Love
Fires up a hotter blaze than Hephaestus kindles on Lipara.*

Learn, lady Moon, how my love came about.

He drives women mad: girls fly in panic from their rooms
And brides desert their still warm marriage beds.'
That is what he said. And I, poor gullible creature,
Took his hand and pulled him down on to my soft bed.
Quickly flesh grew warm against flesh, and our faces   140
Became flushed with heat. We whispered sweet nothings.
There is no need to prolong the tale, dear Moon:
We went to the very end, and both fulfilled our desires.
Neither he nor I had reason to reproach the other,
Till yesterday. But today, as rosy Dawn's horses
Lifted her swiftly from Ocean and raced across the sky,
The mother of Melixo and Philista, our flute-player,
Came to see me. Among the rest of her gossip she said
That Delphis was in love. Whether it was man or woman   150
He desired, she couldn't say for sure; but she did know
He called constantly for unmixed wine*—'To Love!'—then
Rushed away out, claiming he had to cover *that* house
With garlands.* That's what the woman said, and she doesn't lie.
Once he would come to me three or four times a day,
And would often leave his Dorian oil flask here.
But now it's eleven days since I so much as saw him.
Has he forgotten me, and finds his pleasure elsewhere?

But now I shall bind him with these love-charms. If he still
Torments me, I swear by the Fates it's Hades' doors he'll beat
    upon;   160
Such is the power of the noxious drugs I keep in my box,
Whose properties I learnt from an Assyrian stranger.*

Farewell then, lady; turn your horses back to Ocean.
I shall patiently bear my longing, as I have until now.
Farewell, queen Moon with your shining throne, farewell
You stars, you who attend the chariot of tranquil Night.

Idyll 3
The Serenade

I'm off to serenade Amaryllis.* My goats here
Are grazing on the hill; Tityrus is looking after them.
Tityrus, my dear old friend, feed my she-goats,
And take them to the spring. Watch out for that he-goat,
The tawny Libyan, in case he tries to butt you.

O lovely Amaryllis, why do you no longer peep
From your cave* and invite me in? I'm your sweetheart—
Do you really hate me, my bride? Do I look snub-nosed
When I'm close to you, and does my beard stick out?   9
You'll make me hang myself. See, I've brought you ten apples,*
Picked where you told me to pick them. Tomorrow
I'll bring more. Look at me, how sorely my heart aches;
O to be that buzzing bee, and fly into your cave,
Slipping through the ivy and fern you hide behind.
Now at last I know who Love is: a cruel god, surely
Suckled by a lioness* and reared in the wild woods.
His smouldering fires roast me to the very bone.
Your glance is lovely, but you are stone! My dark-browed bride,
Come here to your goatherd's arms so that I can kiss you;
Even in innocent kisses there is sweet delight.   20
And this wreath I wear for you, dear Amaryllis,
Of ivy woven with rosebuds and fragrant wild celery—
You will make me tear it, now, into tiny pieces.
O misery! What will become of me? You don't even listen.
Off with my cloak! I'll plunge in the sea from the cliff
Where Olpis the fisherman watches for shoals of tunny.
Even if that does not kill me, you will be glad.
I wondered the other day if you loved me, and learnt
The truth when the love-in-absence* didn't stick to my smooth

Forearm but shrivelled there, though I smacked it hard.   30
That old crone, too, she that tells fortunes with a sieve,*
Was right. She was gathering herbs nearby, and told me
Though I'm besotted with you, you don't care for me at all.
And yet I am keeping a white she-goat just for you,
With two kids. Mermnon's dusky slave-girl wants them;
Well, she'll have them, and that will teach you to tease me.

My right eye's twitching—does it mean I shall see her?
I'll lean up against this pine tree while I sing,
And maybe she'll look this way; she isn't made of stone.

Hippomenes,* in his eagerness to marry the girl,   40
Picked up the apples and ran the race. Atalanta* saw it,
And in that instant plunged into love,* and was mad.
Down from Othrys the seer Melampus* drove his herd
To Pylos, and so the lovely mother of wise Alphesiboea
Lay at last in the loving arms of Bias.

Adonis,* grazing his sheep on the hills, drove fair Cytherea*
To such a pitch of madness that even after his death
She still refused to put him away from her breast.

Endymion* sleeps undisturbed. How I envy him,   50
And Iasion* too, O my lady, who reaped the reward
That only those who pass through his rites may know.

My head hurts, but that matters nothing to you.
I'll sing no more, but lie here where I've fallen, and wolves
Will eat me up. May that be sweet as honey in your throat.

Idyll 4
The Two Herdsmen

BATTUS Tell me, Corydon, who do those cows belong to?
Philondas?

CORYDON No, they're Aegon's.* He gave them to me to graze.

BATTUS And you secretly milk them all in the evening, I'll bet?

CORYDON No, the old man puts the calves to them then, and
keeps an eye on me.

BATTUS So their master the herdsman has vanished. Where has
he gone?

CORYDON Haven't you heard? Milon's* taken him off to the
River Alpheus.*

BATTUS To Olympia? Since when was Aegon at home in a
wrestling school?

CORYDON They do say he's a match for Heracles in power and
strength.

BATTUS Yes, and my mother always said I could outbox
Polydeuces.*

CORYDON Well, he's taken a shovel and twenty sheep from here
with him.   10

BATTUS I wonder why Milon didn't invite rabid wolves in, if
that's his idea.*

CORYDON Those heifers do miss their master; listen to them
lowing.

BATTUS Poor things! Now they know what a hopeless herdsman
they've got.

CORYDON They certainly are poor things. They have lost the will
to eat.

BATTUS Yes, look at that calf; there's nothing left of her but
bones.
    She doesn't slake her thirst on dewdrops, does she, like a
    cicada?*

CORYDON Lord, no. Sometimes I pasture her by the Aesarus*
        river
    And give her a nice bundle of soft grass, and sometimes
    She plays about on Latymnus,* where the shade is deep.
BATTUS That bull is thin as well—the tawny one. Lampriadas'*
        people   20
    Deserve to have one just like it when they sacrifice to Hera.*
    They are villains, the whole lot of them, in that village.
CORYDON And yet I drive him to the salt-lagoon, and to Physcus'
        land,
    And to the River Neaethus,* where the best plants all grow:
    Restharrow, fleabane, and sweet-smelling balm.
BATTUS Ah, wretched Aegon! Both you and your cows will pass
    To Hades, for you have joined the devotees of cursed victory.
    The pipe which you once fashioned now is flecked with
        mildew.
CORYDON No it is not, not by the Nymphs. As he went off to
        Pisa*
    He left it to me as a present. I can sing a bit, you know,   30
    And can give you the songs of Pyrrhus,* or Glauce's,* well
        enough:
    I sing the praises of Croton*—"A fair town is Zakynthos*
        . . ."—
    And I sing of the Lacinian* shrine that faces the dawn, where
    Aegon the boxer once devoured eighty loaves all by himself.
    It was there that he seized the bull by its hoof, brought it
    Down from the mountain and gave it to Amaryllis.
    The women screamed, and the herdsman laughed out loud.
BATTUS O lovely Amaryllis, of you alone we can say we shall not
    Forget you, even in death. As dear to me as my goats you were
    When you died. Alas for the heavy fate that is my portion.   40
CORYDON Cheer up, Battus my friend. Things may be better
        tomorrow.
    To live is still to hope—it's only the dead who despair.
    Zeus decides: one day it's fine weather, and the next it rains.
BATTUS I'm all right . . . Hey, drive the calves up from down
        there!
    They are nibbling the olive shoots, the greedy beasts.

CORYDON Shoo, Blanche! Shoo, Fruity, up the hill with you!
   Can't you hear me? Get out of there, or you'll come to
   A sticky end, by Pan you will! Look, that one's going back.
   I wish I had a hooked stick, to give you a good poke!

BATTUS Zeus! Look at this, Corydon—*I've* just got a poke*   50
   From a thorn, here below my ankle. These thistles are
   Everywhere. Damn that heifer; it was her I was gaping at
   When the thorn speared me. Can you see it?

CORYDON Yes . . . yes, I've got it between my nails. And here it is!

BATTUS What a tiny wound, and what a mighty man it has
   tamed.

CORYDON You shouldn't go barefoot, Battus, when you're
   roaming the hills;
   Thorns and brambles grow everywhere on the hills.

BATTUS Tell me, Corydon, is the old fellow still screwing
   That dark-browed little tart he once had an itch for?

CORYDON Yes, still at it—didn't you know? At any rate, the other
   day   60
   I caught him actually on the job, down by the cowshed.

BATTUS Good for him, the randy old lecher. He and his family
   Could give satyrs and thin-shanked Pans a close match.

Idyll 5
Goatherd and Shepherd

COMATAS Hey, goats, look out for that shepherd there, Lacon
From Sybaris!* Yesterday he stole my goatskin.

LACON Shoo, lambs, away from that spring! It's Comatas,
Can't you see?—the one who stole my pipe last week.

COMATAS What pipe was that? When did Sibyrtas' slave ever
Get his hands on a pipe? You should stick to tootling
Duets with your friend Corydon on whistles of straw.

LACON Oh, free citizen all of a sudden, are we? The pipe was
A present from Lycon. But what skin was it that Lacon   9
Stole? Not even your master Eumaras owned one to sleep on.

COMATAS Dappled, it was, a gift from Crocylus, when he
Offered the goat to the Nymphs. At the time you were
Eaten up with envy; and now you've left me naked for ever.

LACON Pan of the shore be my witness that Lacon Calaethis' son
Never stripped you of your cloak. If I lie, may I
Go mad and leap from that rock into Crathis'* stream.

COMATAS Well, *my* witnesses are these Nymphs of the lake
(May they always be kindly and gentle to me): Comatas
Never stole up on you and made off with your pipe.

LACON May I suffer the pains of Daphnis* if I believe you.   20
But look here: stake me a kid if you like—not much,
I agree, but we can match song for song, till you give in.

COMATAS A pig once challenged Athena,* they say. All right,
there is
The kid; so come on, now put forward your fat lamb.

LACON Oh you fox! What kind of a bargain is that?
No one shears hair before wool, or milks a bitch
When a goat with her first-born kid stands nearby.

COMATAS Someone who's sure he's going to win does—like you.
Well, wasps may buzz at cicadas.* If you say

One kid's not an equal stake, then here is a goat.   30
Begin the match!

LACON Slow down—you're not on fire.
Come and sit here in this grove, under this olive tree,
And sing in more comfort. Here water drips cool,
There is grass for our couch, and grasshoppers sing.

COMATAS I'm in no hurry; I'm just angry that you have the nerve
To look me straight in the face. I taught you to sing
When you were a boy—and this is kindness' reward.
Rear dogs or wolf cubs, and they'll grow up to eat you.

LACON Did I ever hear or learn a worthwhile lesson from you?
I don't remember. Envious and ugly, that's you to a T.   40

COMATAS Well, you howled when I shafted you; my she-goats'
Bleats mocked you, and the billy gave them a poke.

LACON Oh, you didn't go deep; may your grave be just as shallow,
Old humpback. Still, come here and start your song—your last.

COMATAS No, I won't join you. Over here galingale grows, and
oaks,
And here bees hum with sweet music about their hives.
Here two springs give out chill water, and birds
Chirp on the trees. The shade, too, is deeper than yours
Over there, and cone-showers drop from the pine overhead.

LACON But here you will walk upon lambskins, believe me,   50
And fleeces softer than sleep. Those goatskins of yours
Smell even ranker than you do. And I've two great bowls
Which I shall give to the Nymphs as an offering:
One of white milk, and the other of sweet-tasting oil.

COMATAS But if you come here, you will walk on soft fern
And flowering oregany. For your couch you'll have
Goatskins four times softer than all your skins of lamb.
My offering to Pan will be eight pails of milk,
And eight bowls crammed with honey-filled combs.

LACON Very well—stay there and sing, challenge me from there.
Stick to your oaks, and keep to your own patch.   61
But who'll be our referee? That cowman would do—
You know the man, Lycopas. Perhaps he'll pass nearby.

COMATAS I wouldn't choose *him*. What about that chap,
Over there near you—that one, cutting broom?

Shall we give him a shout? It's Morson the woodsman.
LACON Let's call him.
COMATAS You do it.
LACON Hey, friend!
  Come and listen to us for a while. We have a match on,
  To see who's the best country singer. And, Morson,
  Don't be partial to me when you judge, nor favour *this* man.
COMATAS Right. Morson, my friend, don't show favour to
    Comatas,   70
  Nor yet, as you reverence the Nymphs, incline to *him*.
  Now, this flock here is Sibyrtas', townsman of Thurii,
  And here, my friend, are Eumaras' goats, from Sybaris.
LACON Zeus! Did anyone ask you who owned these flocks?
  Sibyrtas' or mine—what does it matter, you gasbag?
COMATAS I'm only telling the truth, my dear chap; it's not
  My way to boast. It's you who are picking a fight.
LACON Very well. Have your say (if you can) and let's send
  Our friend here back to town with his life. Healer Apollo,
  Comatas, how your mouth runs away with you!

COMATAS More dear to the Muses am I than Daphnis* the singer.
  I sacrificed two goats to them a few days ago.
LACON And *I* am most loved by Apollo. I pasture for him
  A fine ram, in time for the oncoming Carnean* feast.
COMATAS All my goats have borne twins, except two. As I milk,
  My girl eyes me and asks, 'Are you all on your own?'
LACON Indeed? Lacon fills almost twenty baskets with cheese,
  And in flowery meadows he buggers his teenage lad.   89
COMATAS As the goatherd drives his flock by, Clearista pelts him
  With apples,* and, pouting her lips, blows him sweet kisses.
LACON When the shepherd sees Cratidas run to meet him, all
    smiles,
  I am driven insane to see his bright hair curling at his neck.
COMATAS But briar and windflower cannot compete with
  The rose which blooms in its bed by the drystone wall.
LACON True—nor acorn with medlar; the holm-oak gives the
    acorn
  A meagre husk, while the other's covering is sweet.

COMATAS Soon I shall give my girl a ring-dove. It is perching
In the juniper tree, and that is where I'll catch it.

LACON I've a surprise gift, too: when I shear the black ewe
Cratidas will have its soft fleece for a cloak.

COMATAS Shoo! Get away from the olives, you kids! Graze   100
Here, by this sloping hillock, where the tamarisks bloom.

LACON Here, you, Horny and Butter—away from the oaks!
Your pasture is here, to the east, where Whitey is.

COMATAS I have a pail of cypress wood, and a wine-bowl too,
Which Praxiteles* might have made; I save them for my girl.

LACON And I have a dog that tears out wolves' throats, the friend
Of sheep; I'll give it to him, my lad, to hunt wild beasts.

COMATAS Look, locusts are leaping over my fence. Don't nibble
My vines, you wretches, they're dry and won't feed you.

LACON Cicadas, your song goads the reapers to work,
Just as I goad Comatas the goatherd in this contest.   110

COMATAS I hate the thick-tailed vixens which come at evening
To Micon's vineyard and strip all its fruit away.

LACON And I hate the fig-eating beetles, whose squadrons
Swoop on the wind, and gorge on Philtadas' fruit.

COMATAS Don't you remember the time I battered your bum?
How you scowled and wriggled and clung to that oak!

LACON No, I don't recall it— but Eumaras once tied you up
And gave you a good beating here. I remember that.   119

COMATAS Morson, did you catch that? Someone's getting cross.
Best get some squills* from an old woman's grave for
protection.

LACON And, Morson, you see my barbs have reached home.
Haleis*
Grows a good antidote—cyclamen.* Go, and dig some up.

COMATAS If that's true, may the waters of Himera* turn into milk,
Let Crathis redden with wine, and its reeds bear fruit.

LACON *I* say, let Sybaris' streams flow with honey. At dawn
May my girl dip her pail not for water, but for nectar.

COMATAS My goats feed on clover and goatwort. They walk
Upon mastich; they lie down to sleep on arbutus.   129

LACON Bee-balm blooms for my sheep to browse; and solflower
Grows in profusion all around, just like roses.

COMATAS I'm out of love with Alcippa. I gave her the ring-dove
　　But I didn't get kissed by the ears* in return.
LACON But I love Eumedes dearly. I gave him the pipe
　　And he gave me a marvellous kiss in return.
COMATAS Jay versus nightingale, hoopoe challenging swan—
　　It's against nature. Lacon, you're always wanting a fight.

MORSON I order the shepherd to stop.* Comatas, Morson
　　Awards you the lamb. When it's sacrificed to the Nymphs　139
　　Be sure you send Morson a good cut of meat, straight away.
COMATAS By Pan, I will. Now, snort your appreciation, my flock
　　Of kids, and see how I roar in exultant laughter
　　At Lacon the shepherd, now I have won the lamb at last.
　　O, I'll leap sky-high. Be happy, my horned goats:
　　Tomorrow I'll take you and bathe you all in Sybaris' lake.
　　Hey, you, the white one, butting away! If you mount
　　A she-goat before the Nymphs receive their due offering
　　I'll have your balls off. He's at it again! If I don't
　　Cut you, may I be gelded just as Melanthius* was.　　150

Idyll 6
Damoetas and Daphnis

One day, Aratus,* Daphnis the cowherd and Damoetas
Gathered their herd into one place. Damoetas' chin
Was red with down, while the other's beard was just coming.
It was noon in summer, and the two sat down by a spring.
This was their song. Daphnis had made the challenge, so he
  began.

DAPHNIS Polyphemus, Galatea pelts your flock with apples.*
  She calls you a goatherd, and one unhappy in love.
  Poor wretch, you take no notice, but sit and play
  Tunefully on your pipe. Look, now she's pelting
  The dog which goes with you, guarding your sheep.   10
  As it runs on the shore, where the waves break
  With a whisper, its eye is cocked to the sea, and,
  Seeing its image reflected there, it begins to bark.
  Take care it does not snap at the girl's legs,
  Tearing her lovely skin as she comes from the sea.
  Even from there she teases you, and like dry
  Thistledown, parched by summer's heat, she
  Flees if a lover pursues her, and pursues him
  If he flees. She moves her pieces in self-defence;*
  In love, you see, Polyphemus, foul often appears as fair.

Damoetas took up the song from him, and began.   20

DAMOETAS I saw her, by Pan I did, pelting my flock; she did not
  Deceive my single eye, my treasure. (I'll see with it
  Till I die, I pray—and I pray the seer Telemus* will take
  His nasty prophecy home to share with his children.)
  But I can tease her back: I don't look at her, but I say

I'm married to someone else. When she hears this,
She sulks, goes mad, and keeps on peering towards
My caves and flocks from her home in the sea.
I whistled to my dog, too, to bark at her. When I   29
Paid her court, it would lay its chin on her lap and whimper.
Perhaps if I go on like this, and she sees me, she'll send
A go-between. But until she swears that she'll share
My bed on this island, I'll bar the door in her face.
And I'm not as ugly, you know, as men say I am;
Just now I looked at myself in the calm sea, and—
As I judged it—saw two handsome cheeks and this
One handsome eye. The water reflected the gleam
Of my teeth, which were whiter than Parian marble.*
Then I spat three times on my chest, to escape the evil eye,*
Just as instructed by Cotyttaris, the wise old crone.

Damoetas ended his song with a kiss for Daphnis.
He gave him a pipe, and received a flute in return.
Damoetas began to play on the flute, and Daphnis on the pipe,
And at the sound the calves began straight away to frisk
On the soft grass. There was neither victory here, nor defeat.

Idyll 7
The Harvest Festival

There was a time when Eucritus and I were walking
From town to Haleis,* and Amyntas came as well.
Phrasidamus and Antigenes were offering first-fruits*
To Demeter. They were Lycopeus' sons—noble stock,
Reaching back to Clytia and Chalcon* himself,
The one who braced his knee at the rock and caused
The spring Burina* to well up under his foot;
Near it a shady grove was enclosed by elms and poplars,
And roofed by the trees' green-leaved abundance.
Our journey was not half-done, and Brasilas' tomb*   10
Had not yet appeared, when we fell in with a traveller
(The Muses caused this), a good man from Cydonia,*
Lycidas* by name. He was a goatherd, as you would
Guess as soon as you saw him—unmistakably goatherd:
The tawny skin of a thick-haired shaggy goat
Hung from his shoulders, smelling of new-made rennet.
Under that was an ancient shirt, tied in with a
Wide belt. In his right hand he carried a curved stick
Of wild olive wood. Quietly he grinned at me, his eye
Twinkled, and laughter touched his lip as he spoke: 20
'Where are you off to, Simichidas, in the noonday heat,
Bustling along, when even the lizard sleeps in the wall,
And tomb-haunting larks look to find their rest?
Such haste—have you invited yourself to dinner somewhere,
Or to sample a townsman's wine jar? At the pace you're going
The pebbles sing as they spurt from under your boots.'

I answered: 'Lycidas, my friend, all men assert
That among herdsmen and reapers you are by far
The best of pipers. It warms my heart to hear it,

Truly it does, and yet I reckon myself your equal,   30
Or so I fancy. We are on our way to a festival—
Some friends of mine are honouring fair-robed Demeter
With first-fruits from their wealth, since the goddess
Has heaped their threshing floor with grain in plenty.
But look: we share the road and the day, so let us two
Sing country songs by turns, and each may profit the other.
I have a clear voice too, you know, the gift of the Muses.
Men call *me* the best of singers, though I'm not one to be
Quickly persuaded, I assure you. I certainly don't believe
I am yet a rival to mighty Sicelidas* of Samos in song,   40
Nor to Philitas.* I'm but a frog competing with grasshoppers.'
All this was to draw him on; and he in turn replied
With a cheerful laugh, 'I can see you're of the stock that
Zeus creates to speak the truth, so look, I'll stake you my
Stick.* I hate the craftsman who strives to build his house
As high as the topmost peak of Mount Oromedon,*
And I hate those Muses' cockerels who crow vainly
To no effect against the singer who comes from Chios.*
But now, let's begin our country songs, and I shall—
Well, my friend, see if you like this little piece   50
I was labouring over the other day on the hills.

"Ageanax shall have a calm voyage to Mytilene,*
When the Kids* appear in the evening sky and the
South wind chases the sea's waves, and Orion
Sets his foot upon Ocean, if only he saves Lycidas
From Aphrodite's blast; hot desire for him burns me up.
Halcyons* shall soothe the sea's waves, and shall calm
The south wind and the east, which churns the wrack
In the sea's lowest depths—halcyons, most loved of birds by the
Grey-green Nereids,* and those who seek their catch in the sea. 60
As he sails for Mytilene may Ageanax's ship
Enjoy fair weather and bring him safe to harbour.
When that day comes, I'll make myself a garland
Of anise, roses, or stocks, and set it on my head.
I'll ladle out Ptelean* wine from the bowl, and sprawl
By the fire, while beans roast in the embers.

My couch shall be piled elbow-deep with fleabane,
Asphodel, and pliant wild celery. Drinking at ease
I shall remember Ageanax, as I lift the cup
And press my lips even to the dregs. Two shepherds   70
Will play their pipes for me: one from Acharnae, and one
From Lycopa.* Nearby Tityrus will sing how once
Daphnis* the cowherd fell in love with Xenea, and how
The mountain grieved over him, and the oaks
Which grow on the banks of Himera* sang a dirge.
He was wasting away like the snow which melts under
Lofty Haemus or Athos, Rhodope or remote Caucasus.*
He will sing how once the goatherd was shut up alive
In a wide chest,* through a king's high-handed arrogance;
In his fragrant cedar chest he was fed by snub-nosed bees,   80
Who came from the meadows to bring him tender flowers,
Because the Muse had poured sweet nectar over his mouth.
O Comatas, long gone! These pleasures were yours:
A chest was your prison, too; you too were fed
On honeycombs while you toiled through the year's springtime.
I wish you had been on earth in my lifetime;
I would have pastured your fine goats on the hills,
Listening to your voice, while you, divine Comatas, lying at ease
Under oaks or pines sang your honey-sweet song." '

Here he ended his song. Then I answered him, and said,   90
'Lycidas, my friend, I too have learned much from the Nymphs
As I grazed my cows on the hills: excellent songs,
Whose fame perhaps has reached the throne of Zeus.*
This is the best of them by far—so listen, please, while I
Begin to pay you honour, for you are dear to the Muses.

"The Loves sneezed for Simichidas;* so he, poor wretch,
Yearns as much for Myrto as goats yearn for the spring.
But as for Aratus,* my dearest friend of all, he desires
A boy, deep in his entrails. Aristis* knows all this—
A good man, the best of men; Phoebus* himself   100
Would allow him into his sanctuary, to sing to his lyre—
How Aratus burns in his bones with love for the boy.

O Pan, patron of Homole's* lovely plains, I beg you, bring
Him unsummoned and press him into my friend's arms,
Whether it is dainty Philinus* or yet some other lad.
Pan, if you bring this about, may your back and shoulders
Be spared a beating with squills by the boys of Arcadia,*
When they are short of game. But if you refuse,
May you scratch yourself all over, covered in bites,
And may you go to your rest on a bed of nettles.   110
Midwinter shall find you on Edonian mountains,*
On your way to the Hebrus,* close by the North Pole.
May Ethiopia's* marches be your summer pasture,
Under the Blemyan* cliff, beyond sight of the Nile.
But you, O Loves, with cheeks as rosy as apples,
Leave the sweet waters of Byblis and Hyetis, and Oecus,*
Shrine of golden-haired Dione.* Wound, I pray you,
Desirable Philinus with your arrows. Wound him,
Since he, cruel boy, can find no pity for my friend.
He is ripe, riper than a pear, and women shout after him   120
'Ah, Philinus, your beauty's bloom is fading away!'
So, Aratus, let us abandon guard duty at his door,
And give our feet a rest. Let the morning cockcrow
Rouse someone else to numbing pain. It's Molon's turn,
And his alone, my friend, to be caught in *that* headlock.
All we should hope for is a tranquil life, and an old crone
To spit* on us and keep all nastiness away." '

I finished my song; and he, with a cheerful laugh as before,
Gave me the stick, pledging friendship in the Muses,
Then slanted off to the left, taking the road to Pyxa.*   130
Eucritus and I and pretty Amyntas turned aside
To the farm of Phrasidamus, where we sank down
With pleasure on deep-piled couches of sweet rushes,
And vine leaves freshly stripped from the bush.
Above us was the constant quiet movement of elm
And poplar, and from the cave of the Nymphs nearby
The sacred water ran with a bubbling sound as it fell.
Soot-black cicadas chattered relentlessly on
Shady branches, and the muttering of tree-frogs

Rose far off from the impenetrable thorn bush.   140
Larks and finches were singing, the turtle-dove moaned,
And bees hummed and darted about the springs.
Everything smelt of the rich harvest, smelt of the fruit-crop.
Apples and pears rolled all around us, enclosing
Our bodies with plenty; branches reached to the ground,
Bent with the weight of plums. Men broke for us
Four-year-old seals from the mouths of their wine jars.
O Nymphs of Castalia,* haunters of steep Parnassus,
Was it such a bowl as this that the old man Chiron*
Set before Heracles in the rocky cave of Pholus?   150
Was it nectar like this that once on Anapus'* banks
Impelled that shepherd, the mighty Polyphemus,
The one who bombarded ships with mountains, to
Dance about his sheepfolds? This was the wine, Nymphs,
You mixed for us on that day, by the altar of Demeter,
Queen of the threshing-floor. May I once again
Plant the great winnowing-fan* in her heap of grain,
While she smiles, her hands laden with poppies and sheaves.*

Idyll 10
The Reapers

MILON Bucaeus, my poor old mate, now what's the matter?
    You don't cut your swathe as straight as you did,
    And you can't keep up with the next reaper; you lag
    Behind, as a ewe with a thorn in her foot trails the flock.
    You haven't made much of a bite into your row;
    How will you last until evening—or afternoon, come to that?
BUCAEUS Milon, you're a chip off a hard rock, and could work till
    dusk,
    I know. Have you never longed for someone far away?
MILON Never. What has longing for other things to do with a
    working man?
BUCAEUS Has it never happened that love gave you a sleepless
    night?   10
MILON I should hope not. When a dog tastes offal,* he's hooked
    on it.
BUCAEUS Well, *I'm* in love, Milon, and it's nearly ten days now . . .
MILON Wine from the cask,* I see; mine is sour, and not much of
    it.
BUCAEUS . . . So the field before my door is all unhoed* since I
    sowed it.
MILON So—which of the girls is it who is torturing you?
BUCAEUS Polybotas' lass, the one
    Who played her pipe for the reapers at Hippocion's farm that
    day.
MILON God finds out the wicked. You've wanted this for a long
    time
    And now you've got it: a skinny insect to cuddle in the night.
BUCAEUS Don't mock me. Wealth's not the only god* who's
    blind.
    There's careless Love as well; so don't talk so big.   20

MILON Oh, I'm not. Look, just lay your sheaves on the ground,
　　　And give us a love song in honour of your girl. It will make
　　　Your work easier to bear. And anyway, you were once a singer.
BUCAEUS Muses of Pieria,* celebrate with me this slender girl
　　　In song. Whatever you touch you make more lovely.

　　　'Beautiful Bombyca, men call you Syrian, thin
　　　And sunburnt. To me alone your skin is pale honey.
　　　The violet is dark, and so is the printed orchid,*
　　　But they are the flowers that men prize most for garlands.
　　　Goats yearn for clover, the wolf pursues the goat.   30
　　　Cranes follow the plough, and I am mad for you.
　　　O to have Croesus' fabled wealth,* to dedicate
　　　Our two selves as golden statues to Aphrodite:
　　　You with a flute in your hand, or a rose, or an apple,
　　　And I in brand new clothes and smart new shoes.
　　　Lovely Bombyca, with your knucklebone feet and flowerlike
　　　Voice, and your winning ways I cannot frame in words.'

MILON Well! This man is a skilful poet, and we never noticed it.
　　　How well he has married his verse to his musical scale.*   39
　　　My beard shows I'm older than you, but I'm not a whit wiser.
　　　Still, divine Lityerses'* songs are also worth a glance. Try this:

　　　'Demeter, generous giver of fruit and grain, may this
　　　Harvest be easily gathered and abound in fruit.
　　　Binders, truss up your sheaves. Let no passer-by say
　　　"What feeble workers these are—more wasted wages!"
　　　Your swathe's cut end should look to the north wind
　　　Or the west; that's how the ear of grain grows ripe.
　　　When you thresh the corn, avoid a midday sleep;
　　　That is the time the grain best breaks from the stalk.
　　　Reapers should start with the waking lark and stop   50
　　　When it sleeps, but rest when the day's heat is fierce.
　　　Pray for a frog's life, lads; he doesn't need a waiter
　　　To pour his drink, since it's all on tap around him.
　　　Boil up those lentils properly, steward, and don't be mean;
　　　Slicing cumin seeds* can lead to a nasty gash in the hand.'

That's what men should sing when they work in the sun.
As for your stringy love,* Bucaeus—turn it into a tale to tell
Your mother when she wakes in bed in the morning.

Idyll 11
The Cyclops' Serenade

Nicias,* there is no remedy for love, no liniment,
As I believe, nor any balm, except the Muses.
Theirs is a gentle, painless drug, and in men's power
To use; but it is hard to find. You know this well,
I think; you are a doctor, and one whom the nine
Muses love above all. This at any rate was the way
My countryman* the Cyclops eased his pain,
Polyphemus long ago, when he loved Galatea,
When the down was fresh about his mouth and temples.
He loved, not with apples, roses, or curls of hair,*   10
But in an outright frenzy. For him, nothing else existed.
Often his flocks would come of their own accord
Back from green pastures to the fold, while he, alone
On the weed-strewn shore, would sing of Galatea from
Break of day, wasting away with love. Deep inside he bore
A cruel wound, which mighty Cypris' dart* had driven
Into his heart. But he found out the cure: he would sit
On some high rock, and gazing out to sea would sing:

'O my white Galatea, why do you spurn your lover?
Whiter to look at than cream cheese, softer than a lamb,   20
More playful than a calf, sleeker than the unripe grape.
Why do you only come just as sweet sleep claims me,
Why do you leave me just as sweet sleep lets me go,
Flying like a ewe at the sight of a grey wolf?
I fell in love with you, my sweet, when first you came
With my mother* to gather flowers of hyacinth
On the mountain, and I was your guide. From the day
I set eyes on you up to this moment, I've loved you
Without a break; but you care nothing, nothing at all.

I know, my beautiful girl, why you run from me: 30
A shaggy brow spreads right across my face
From ear to ear in one unbroken line. Below is a
Single eye, and above my lip is set a broad flat nose.
Such may be my looks, but I pasture a thousand beasts,
And I drink the best of the milk I get from them.
Cheese too I have in abundance, in summer and autumn,
And even at winter's end; my racks are always laden.
And I can pipe better than any Cyclops here,
When I sing, my sweet pippin, deep in the night
Of you and me. For you I'm rearing eleven fawns,   40
All marked on their necks, and four bear cubs too.
O please, come. You will see that life is just as good
If you leave the grey-green sea behind to crash on the shore,
And at night you will find more joy in this cave with me.
Here there are bays, and here slender cypresses,
Here is sombre ivy, and here the vine's sweet fruit;
Here there is ice-cold water which dense-wooded Etna
Sends from its white snows—a drink fit for the gods.
Who could prefer waves and the sea to all this?
But if you think I'm a touch too hairy for you,   50
I have oak logs here, and under the ash unflagging fire.
Burn away my life with fire—I could bear even that,
And my single eye,* my one dearest possession of all.
I wish my mother had given me gills when I was born,
Then I could have dived down and kissed your hand,
If you denied me your mouth, and brought you white
Snowdrops or delicate poppies with their scarlet petals.
One grows in summer and the other grows in winter,
So you see I could not bring you both at once.
It's not too late, my sweet, for me to learn to swim;*   60
If only some mariner* would sail here in his ship,
Then I could fathom why you nymphs love life in the deep.
Come out, Galatea, come out and forget your home,
Just as I sit here and forget to return to mine.
Follow the shepherd's life with me—milking,
And setting cheese with the rennet's pungent drops.
It's my mother who does me wrong; it's her alone I blame.

She's not once spoken a gentle word to you about me,
Although she sees me wasting away, day by day.
I'll see she knows how my head and feet throb with pain, 70
So that her torment will be equal to what I suffer.

O Cyclops, Cyclops, where have your wits flown away?
Show some sense, go and weave some baskets, collect
Green shoots for your lambs. Milk the ewe
At hand;* why chase the one who runs away? Maybe
You'll find another Galatea, and a prettier one too.
I'm invited out for night-time play by lots of girls,
And they giggle together as soon as they see I've heard.
On land I too am clearly a man of some consequence.'

So by singing the Cyclops shepherded* his love, 80
And more relief it brought him than paying a large fee.*

Idyll 12
The Beloved

My dear lad, you have come! Two days and nights
Have passed, but now you have come! One day is long
Enough for lovers to age. As the spring is sweeter
Than winter, as apple than sloe, as the ewe is thicker-
Fleeced than her lamb, as the virgin eclipses the thrice-wed
Woman, as fawn is swifter than calf, and the clear-voiced
Nightingale's musical song is beyond all birds';
So has your return warmed me, and I ran as a
Traveller seeks the oak's shade in the burning sun.
How I wish the Loves might breathe an equal passion   10
Into us both, so that future men might sing of us:
'These were two famous men in former times—
One the "Inspirer"* (as the speech of Amyclae has it)
And one the "Listener" (as they say in Thessaly).
They were yoked in mutual love. Then indeed was the
Golden Age restored, when the loved one loved in return.'
May it be, O may it be, Zeus and you ageless immortals:
When two hundred generations have passed, may a
Messenger come to me by Acheron,* river of no return, and say:
'Men still speak of your love, and the love of the   20
Graceful Listener—and the young men most of all.'
The gods in heaven will bring all this to pass,
If they choose. But as for me, no pimples* will grow
On my narrow nose if I celebrate your beauty.
If sometimes you hurt me, you heal it straight away.
My cup spills over, because you have doubled my joy.
May your lives be blessed, Megarians of Nisaea,* champion
Oarsmen, because you bestowed a signal honour
On Diocles* the Athenian stranger, lover of boys.
Every year at the start of spring young men gather   30

Around his tomb, and compete for a prize in kissing.
The one who plants the sweetest kisses, lip on lip,
Goes home to his mother bowed with the weight of garlands.
Happy the man chosen to judge these boys' kisses!
He must send fervent prayers to glorious Ganymede*
For a mouth as accurate as that Lydian touchstone*
Which moneychangers use to test true gold from false.

Idyll 13
The Story of Hylas

Love was not born for us alone, as once we thought,
Nicias, whichever god it was who fathered him.*
We were not the first to be beguiled by beauty,
We who are mortal, and cannot see tomorrow.
No, even Amphitryon's son,* whose heart was bronze,
And who withstood the savage lion,* loved a boy,
Beautiful Hylas, whose hair was still unshorn.
Just as father to son, Heracles taught him the lessons
Which had brought him nobility and renown in song.
They were never apart, neither at noonday nor   10
When Dawn's white horses flew up into the sky,
Or when clucking chickens looked to their rest
While their mother shook her wings on her soot-black perch.
Thus he hoped the boy would be trained after his own mind,
And by his efforts reach the state of true manhood.

And so, when Jason,* son of Aeson, sailed in search of the
Golden Fleece, and noble heroes from every city
Went with him, a picked company with skills to offer,
There also came to wealthy Iolcus* the man of many labours,
The son of Alcmena, who was princess of Midea.*   20
With him Hylas went down to the strong-benched Argo,
The ship which sped past the gloomy clashing rocks*
Ungrazed, and shot between to the huge expanse
Of the deep gulf of Phasis,* just like an eagle.
And from that day till now the rocks have stood unmoved.

It was at the Pleiads' rising,* at the time when lambs graze
On the margin land and spring has turned into summer,
That the godlike band of heroes turned their minds
To their voyage. They took their seats in the hollow

Argo, and with three days' south wind astern
Reached the Hellespont, and anchored in Propontis,*   30
Where the Cianian* people's oxen trace broad furrows
With the bright ploughshare. They disembarked,
And made their evening meal on the beach in pairs;
But they prepared one sleeping-place for all, because
There was a great store of stuff for their beds: a meadow,
Where they cut sharp sedge and ample galingale.

Golden-haired Hylas went to fetch water in a bronze
Jug, for the meal of Heracles and steadfast Telamon,*
Since the two friends always messed together. Soon he saw
A spring in a hollow; around it grew abundant reeds,   40
Fresh green maidenhair and dark blue celandine,
Carpets of wild celery, and creeping dogstooth grass.
In the water Nymphs were preparing to dance,
Sleepless divine Nymphs, feared by country folk—
Eunica and Malis, and Nychea* with spring in her eyes.
As the boy reached down in haste to dip his capacious
Pitcher into the pool, they all seized his hand,
Their tender hearts driven to madness with desire
For the Argive boy.* Down he fell with a rush
Into the dark pool, just as a shooting star falls   50
With a rush into the sea, and a sailor calls to his mates:
'Ease your ropes out, lads: it's a sailing wind!'
The weeping boy was cushioned on the Nymphs' laps,
As they tried to comfort him with soothing words.

But Amphitryon's son, disturbed at the boy's delay,
Set off holding his bow with the Scythian curve*
And the club he always grasped in his right hand.
'Hylas!' he bellowed, as loud as his deep throat could cry,
Three times.* Three times the boy replied, but his voice
Rose faint from the pool; though close, it sounded far away. 60
The flesh-eating lion hears a fawn calling in the hills
And bounds from its lair to seek out a ready feast;
So did Heracles rampage through untrodden thorn-brakes,
Covering vast tracts of land, in longing for the boy.
How reckless lovers are! How he suffered, as he roamed

Over hills and through forests, and Jason's expedition
Went clean from his mind. The ship lay ready, with gear aloft,
But then at midnight the heroes stowed the sails away,
And waited for Heracles; but he was crazed, and wandered   70
Where his feet took him, his heart torn by a cruel god.

And so handsome Hylas is counted among the immortals.
Heracles was mocked by the heroes, and called a deserter,
Because he abandoned Argo, the ship of thirty benches,
And came on foot to Colchis and inhospitable Phasis.*

Idyll 14
Aeschinas and Thyonichus

AESCHINAS Good day to you, Thyonichus my friend.

THYONICHUS And the same to you, Aeschinas.
It's been a long time.

AESCHINAS It has.

THYONICHUS What's the matter?

AESCHINAS Things aren't too good with me.

THYONICHUS Ah, that's why you're so thin—you need a good
    shave, and your hair's
All long and scraggy! A Pythagorist* was here the other day,
    looking
Just like you, pale and barefoot. An Athenian,* he said he was.

AESCHINAS So he too was in love?

THYONICHUS Yes—with best wheat bread, I thought.

AESCHINAS Very funny, my friend, as usual. No, It's lovely
    Cynisca—she's
Making a fool of me. One day I shall go crazy, just like that.
Only a hair's breadth separates me from madness, you know.

THYONICHUS You're always the same, Aeschinas—a bit the
    impulsive type,   10
And you want everything to be just so. Still, tell me your news.

AESCHINAS We were having a drink at my place, in the country—
That chap from Argos, and Agis the Thessalian trainer,*
Cleunicus the soldier, and me. I'd killed a sucking pig and a
Brace of chickens, and opened some Bibline wine*
For them: four years old, but its bouquet was almost as fine
As when it came from the vat. I had produced
An onion or two,* and some snails. It was a good party.
As time went on, we decided that everyone
Should toast his loved one in neat wine;* only
He had to say who it was. So we went on drinking   20

And naming, as agreed; but *she* said nothing, though
I was present. What do you think I thought of that?
Then someone joked, 'Have you been struck dumb?
Seen a wolf?'* 'How clever of you,' she said, and blushed—
You could have easily lighted a lamp from her cheek.
There *is* a wolf, you see, my neighbour Labes' son Wolf:
Tall, smooth-skinned, and handsome—or so many people
   think.
He was the one who'd ignited her *grande passion.*
I'd heard about the affair, just by the way, but I hadn't
Followed it up. So much for being grown-up and having a
   beard.
Anyway, the four of us by now were pretty far gone, when
The man from Larisa* sang 'O Wolf, My Wolf' from end to
   end—   30
Some Thessalian song, the brute. Then Cynisca suddenly
Burst into floods of tears, worse than a six-year-old girl
Wailing for her mother's lap. So then I—you know me,
What I'm like—I gave her a smack on the head, and then
I did it again. She picked up her dress and fled
Outside. 'You bitch,' I said, 'so I'm not good enough?
Have you got another sweetheart? All right, go and cuddle
Your new friend. If you're crying for *him* you can
Let your tears come in drops as big as apples.'
A swallow brings titbits for her young under the eaves,
And then is off like a flash to get more food for them.   40
Well, Cynisca flew from her soft seat faster than any swallow,
Straight through the yard and out—any escape would do.
'The bull once fled to the wood',* as the proverb says.

Let's see: twenty days, then eight, nine, ten more, and today's
The eleventh. Add two, and that's two months we've been
   apart.
I could have a Thracian haircut,* and she wouldn't know.
It's all Wolf now, and the door's open for Wolf, even at night.
I don't count, she doesn't think of me, I'm just like the poor
Megarians, stuck at the foot of the league.* Now, if I could
Fall out of love, that would certainly help. But as it is,   50
How can I? Like the mouse in the tale, I'm tasting pitch,*

And I don't know the cure for helpless love. But wait:
Simus loved a girl as hard as bronze, and he went to sea,
And came back cured. He was about my age; I'll take
Ship as well. A soldier's life is not the worst on offer,
Perhaps, nor yet the best, but it serves well enough.

THYONICHUS I wish things had turned out the way you wanted
    them,
    Aeschinas. But if you're really set on going abroad,
    Ptolemy's the best paymaster a free man could have.

AESCHINAS Apart from that, what's he like?

THYONICHUS The best: quite the most   60
    Gracious and amiable of men, a lover of arts and women.*
    He can recognize a friend—and an enemy even better.
    He's very generous, too, and won't turn down a request—
    As you would expect in a king—though it isn't wise
    To keep on asking, Aeschinas. So if you fancy pinning
    Your cloak on your right shoulder,* resolved to stand
    On both feet to meet a fearless enemy's charge,* then it's
    Egypt for you—pronto. None of us is getting younger, and
    Whitening time creeps steadily from temple to cheek.
    We should make our mark while there's still spring in our
        knees.   70

Idyll 15
The Women at the Festival

The House

GORGO Praxinoa at home?

PRAXINOA She is! Gorgo, dear, it's been such a long time!
  I'm surprised you made it even now. Eunoa, a chair for the
    lady,
  And put a cushion on it.

GORGO I'm fine, thanks.

PRAXINOA Do sit down.

GORGO What a dreadful state I'm in! I scarcely got here alive,
  Such a huge crowd, racing chariots everywhere, and the
  Military all over the place, with their great boots and cloaks.
  And the road is endless—every time your house is farther
    away.

PRAXINOA That's my demented husband. He went and took this
  End-of-the-world place, a hovel, not a house, just so that
  You and I should not be neighbours. It's just to spite me,
  The selfish beast—but that's what he's like all the time. 10

GORGO Don't speak of your husband Dinon, dear, like that,
  In front of the little one. Look at him gazing at you.
  Never mind, Zopyrion sweetie, she doesn't mean daddy.

PRAXINOA Good heavens, the child understands you.

GORGO He's a nice daddy!

PRAXINOA That's as may be. This daddy the other day—
  It was the other day I said to him, 'Papa, go and buy me
  Some soda and some red dye from the shops.'
  And what did he bring me back? Salt, the big booby.

GORGO Mine's just the same: Diocleidas annihilates money.
  Yesterday he spent seven drachmas on—well, dog hairs,
  Shreds from old skin bags, total rubbish: five fleeces,

And all extra work for me. Anyway, come on, get   20
Your dress and wrap; we're going to see the *Adonis*
In rich King Ptolemy's palace. I hear the queen
Is planning a splendid show.
PRAXINOA Those who have it can flaunt it.
GORGO But when you've seen it you can tell the others who
    haven't.
Time to go.
PRAXINOA Life's all holiday for those with nothing to do.
Eunoa, take that spinning away. Leave it lying about
And you'll catch it; cats like a soft bed. Go on, move!
Quick, bring some water. I need the water first,
So she brings soap. Give me it anyway. Not too much,   30
You lazy slut. Now pour the water. You fool, you're soaking
My blouse. That will do. I've washed enough for the gods.*
Where's the key to the big chest? Bring it to me.
GORGO That pleated dress really suits you, Praxinoa. Tell me,
How much did the cloth cost you, off the loom?
PRAXINOA Don't remind me. More than two hundred drachmas
In hard cash. I put my heart and soul into the embroidery.
GORGO Well, it's turned out well on you, you must agree.
PRAXINOA Bring me my wrap and my sun hat. Arrange them
    nicely.
I'm not taking you, child. Nasty witch,* horsey bites!   40
Cry as much as you like, I'm not having you
Kicked lame. Let's go. Phrygia, take the baby and
Play with him, call the dog in, and lock the outer door.

The Street

Ye gods, what a crush! How can we get through this rabble?
We'll be late. They're like ants—impossible to count.
You've done much good, Ptolemy, since your father went
    immortal:*
Villains don't creep up on you now in the street and mug you
Egyptian fashion*—that was a dirty game they used to play,
Ruffians to a man, born criminals. To hell with the lot of them.

Dearest Gorgo, what will become of us? Look at the king's
  horses!   51
Don't tread on me, my good man! That chestnut's rearing up,
Look how wild it is. Watch out, Eunoa, you silly girl!
It'll kill its minder. What a good thing I left the baby at home.

GORGO Cheer up, Praxinoa. Look, we're behind them. They've
  gone
To their places.

PRAXINOA I'm all right again now. Ever since I was
A child, what I've been most afraid of are a horse and
A cold snake. Let's get on; this great mob is swamping us.

GORGO Have you come from the palace, mother?   60

OLD WOMAN I have, children.

GORGO Well, is it easy to get in?

OLD WOMAN The Greeks entered Troy by trying,*
Pretty children. If you try, everything comes to pass.

GORGO The old dear speaks in riddles, like a prophet. Now she's
  gone.

PRAXINOA Oh, women know everything, even how Zeus married
  Hera.*

GORGO Praxinoa, look; what an enormous crush there is around
  the doors.

PRAXINOA Incredible. Gorgo, give me your hand. Eunoa, you
  hold
Eutychis', and make sure you don't wander away from her.
We'll all go in together. Stay close to us, Eunoa.
Oh *no*—look, Gorgo, my dress is quite torn in two.
In Zeus' name, man, will you please mind my wrap!   70

STRANGER It's not my fault; but I'll try as hard as I can.

PRAXINOA What a scrum! They are shoving each other like pigs.

STRANGER Cheer up, lady, we're all right now.

PRAXINOA Well, sir, you'll be in my debt
For ever, for looking after us. *(To Gorgo)* What a nice kind man.
Eunoa's being squashed against us. Go on, push, you coward!
That's better. 'All the women inside',* as the man said
When he locked the door on the bride.

The Palace

GORGO Praxinoa, come over here and look at these beautiful
 tapestries:
 So delicate and pretty—clothes fit for the gods, you'd say.
PRAXINOA Lady Athena,* to think of the weaving that went into
 them!   80
 Such artists, to make their designs appear so true to life.
 How naturally the figures stand, how naturally they move!
 They seem alive, not woven. Ah, what a clever creature man is!
 And how wonderfully *he* reclines on his silver couch,
 With the first downy growth spreading from his temples:
 Thrice-adored Adonis, adored even beside Acheron.*
SECOND STRANGER Do stop it, you silly creatures, twittering
 endlessly, cooing
 Like doves. They'll exhaust me with their great broad vowels.*
PRAXINOA Oh, where's *he* from, then? What's our twittering to
 you?
 We're not your slaves; it's Syracusans you're bossing about. 90
 And listen: we're from Corinth* way back, like Bellerophon,
 So we talk Peloponnesian.* Dorians may speak Dorian, I
 presume?
 Persephone, grant us to have no master—except one, that is.*
 Anyway, I don't care. Don't waste your time bullying me.
GORGO Hush, Praxinoa, she's going to sing the *Song of Adonis*—
 The Argive woman's daughter, that brilliant singer, the one
 Who won the prize last year in the lament. She'll put on
 A good performance, I'm sure. Listen, she's clearing her
 throat.

THE SINGER Mistress, you who love Golgi, sheer Eryx and
 Idalium,*   100
 Aphrodite, whose sport is golden. See how after a year
 The soft-footed Hours* have brought you back Adonis from
 Ever-flowing Acheron—the dear Hours, slowest of the gods,
 Yet all men long for them, for they always bring some gift.
 Cypris,* Dione's child, you made mortal Berenice* an
 immortal,

So men say, sprinkling ambrosia on to her woman's breast.
And so in your honour, many-shrined and many-named
    goddess,
Arsinoa, daughter of Berenice, who resembles Helen,*   110
Now pampers Adonis with delights of every kind.
Before him are laid in season the burden of fruit trees,
And delicate plants preserved in baskets of silver,
And Syrian perfume in jars of gold. Cakes, too, such as
Women knead, by mixing all manner of colours with
White wheat flour; and others of sweet honey and moist oil.
All creatures that inhabit the air and the earth attend him.
Beside him there are fashioned fresh green bowers, heavy with
Soft dill. Boy Loves fly above, like fledgling nightingales   120
Swooping from branch to branch as they try out their wings.
O gold, O ebony, O eagles of white ivory that carry off
To Zeus the son of Cronos a boy to pour his wine.*
And the couch's red coverlets, softer than sleep! Milesian
    women*
And shepherds of Samos will say, '*We* made the coverlets
For beautiful Adonis' couch.' Cypris embraces him
In her arms, and Adonis' rosy arms hold her. The groom
Is eighteen, nineteen; his kisses do not prick her,
For his lip is covered with nothing but reddish down.   130

Now farewell to Cypris, who holds her lover in her arms.
At dawn, with the dew, we shall bear him in a group
Down to where the waves splash on the shore. Then, with
Our hair flowing free, breasts bare, and our dresses sweeping
Our ankles, we shall strike up the clear and piercing song.*

Dear Adonis, you alone of all other demigods, men say, haunt
Both this world and Acheron.* Fate would not grant
    Agamemnon*
This gift, nor great Ajax, that hero heavy in anger, nor
    Hector,*
Eldest of Hecabe's twenty sons; not Patroclus, nor Pyrrhus*
Returned from Troy, nor even the Lapiths of old, nor
    Deucalion*   141
And his people; nor the descendants of Pelops,* nor the

Pelasgian kings of Argos.* Be gracious to us, dear Adonis,
Again next year. This year's visitation made us joyful,
And when you come again you will find a welcome.

GORGO She is such a clever creature, that woman, Praxinoa:
Lucky to know so much, and luckier still to have
Such a lovely voice. But it's time to go home—Diocleidas
Has not had his lunch, and he has a sharp temper; it's best to
Leave him alone when he's hungry. Be happy, beloved Adonis,
And may you find *us* happy when you come back here again.

Idyll 16
The Graces

The constant task of the daughters of Zeus, and of poets,
Is to celebrate in song the immortals and the glorious
Deeds of heroes. Muses are goddesses, and therefore sing of gods;
We on earth are mortal, so let us sing of mortal men.

Is there a man living under the bright sky, who will gladly
Open his house to my Graces* and entertain them, instead of
Sending them back on their way without a gift? These days
They slink home barefoot, angry and grumbling at me
Because I have sent them on a pointless journey. Back in their
Empty box they go, and crouch in its depths, their heads   10
Drooped on their cold knees. This is always their refuge
When they return home from a useless errand. Will anyone
Nowadays treat them well? Is there anyone who values
The poet who has sung his praises? I do not know. In times
Gone by men sought praise for glorious deeds. No more:
Enslaved by greed, they hide their hands under their cloaks,
On the watch for a chance to make yet more cash, grudging even
The rust from their coins. Instead the quick reply comes back,
'Charity begins at home', 'I'm only a poor man myself', or
'Who needs more poets? Homer's enough'; 'Gods look after   20
Poets'; 'The only good poet's one who costs me nothing'.

I ask you, gentlemen: what is the point of hoarding masses of
    gold?
Wealth, says the man of sense, should be used to indulge
Yourself—and after that, perhaps, to give the poet a little;
To do a good turn to one's relations, and to others, as far
As you can; to offer regular gifts on the gods' altars;
To be a generous and kindly host, not sending your guest from

Your table until he's ready to go; but above all, to honour the
    Muses'
Priestly interpreters, so that men may speak well of you
Even when you're hidden deep in Hades. Do this, and you won't
Be forced to grieve without honour on Acheron's* chill banks,   31
Like a poor man, his hands callused by the spade's toil,
Who complains at his inheritance of helpless poverty.

Many were the peasants who drew their rationed dole
Month by month in the halls of the kings Aleuas and Antiochus;*
Many the calves and horned cattle which were herded
Lowing to the byres belonging to the sons of Scopas;
Prize sheep in their thousands were grazed by shepherds on the
Plain of Crannon,* all owned by the hospitable house of Creon.
Yet none of these gained enjoyment from their wealth, when
    once   40
They had emptied their sweet lives out, on to the gloomy
    ferryman's
Broad raft. Parted from their huge fortunes, they would have lain
Forgotten for time beyond reckoning among the luckless dead,
Had not the poet of Ceos shaped inventive songs to his
Lyre of many strings, establishing their fame among men
To come. Even their swift horses,* who brought them victory
Crowns from the sacred games, received their share of honour.
Who would ever have heard of the champions of Lycia,*
Or Priam's long-haired sons, or Cycnus* and his womanish skin,
If poets had not sung of the battle-cries of men of old?   50
For ten long years Odysseus wandered throughout the world,
    reached
Remote Hades alive, and escaped from the murderous Cyclops'
    cave;
But everlasting fame would have passed him by, and silence too
Would have shrouded Eumaeus* the swineherd, and Philoetius
Bustling about his cattle herds, and even the generous Laertes,*
Had not the songs of an Ionian* brought them the reward of
    fame.

It is through the Muses that men win good reputation;
Men's wealth is wasted by their heirs when they are dead.

This truth is lost on those corrupted by greed; as well
Labour in vain to count the waves on the beach when wind   60
And grey-green sea drive them on to shore, or try to wash
A muddy brick in clear water. Well, good luck to misers:
May their wealth increase beyond measure, may they stay
   enslaved
To their desire for even more. As for me, I prefer reputation
And men's friendship to wealth reckoned in mules and horses;

My search is for a man who will welcome me, and my Muses too,
For the poet travels a hard road when unaccompanied
By the daughters of Zeus the mighty Counsellor. Heaven   70
Is not yet weary of bringing round the months and years,
And many more times will its horses start up the wheels of day.
One day there will come a man who will need my poet's art,
Someone who has matched the deeds of great Achilles, or of
Grim Ajax on the plain of Simois* by the tomb of Phrygian Ilus.
Even now the Phoenicians* who inhabit the farthest tracts
Of Libya,* under the setting sun, are shuddering in fear;
Even now the people of Syracuse are gripping their spears
At the midpoint and hefting their heavy wicker shields.
In among them Hieron arms himself like a hero from   80
Days gone by, his helmet shadowed by a horsehair crest.
To you, O glorious father Zeus and lady Athena, and to you,
Maiden,* with your mother patron of the wealthy Ephyraeans,
Whose city lies near the waters of Lysimeleia,* I now pray:
May harsh compulsion drive our enemies from this island
Over the Sardinian sea, to bring hard news to wives
And children about their loved ones' deaths, and may
These messengers be but a fraction left from the invading army.
May the cities which enemy hands have cruelly razed
Be once again peopled by their former inhabitants.
May rich harvests repay their toil, and may sheep in their   90
Countless thousands fatten in pastures, bleating across
The plain; and may herds of cattle as they wander back
To their folds quicken the evening traveller's steps.
May fallow land be ploughed again, ready for seed-time,
At the season when the cicada, keeping watch over shepherds
In the noonday sun, sings loudly high up in the tree branches.

May their armour be covered with spiders' fine-spun webs, and
Even the name of the battle-cry be forgotten. May singers exalt
Hieron's glory aloft, across the Scythian* sea to the wide
Pitch-packed battlements* where Semiramis once was queen. 100

I am simply one among many loved by the daughters of Zeus;
May every poet resolve to sing of Sicilian Arethusa,*
Her army of citizens, and Hieron, the renowned spearman.
O goddess Graces, loved by Eteocles,* and dear to
Minyan Orchomenus* (once the enemy of Thebes):
If no one summons me I shall stay at home, but I shall
Gladly go to the house of the man who calls me, taking my Muses
With me. Nor shall I forget *you*, my Graces—what joy is there
For men without you? May I always live in the Graces' company.

Idyll 17
In Praise of Ptolemy

From Zeus let us begin, Muses, and with Zeus let us end,
When we make our songs, for he is pre-eminent among the gods.
But among mortals, let Ptolemy be reckoned first,
First and last and in between, for he is supreme among men.
Heroes of former times, children of demigods, had skilful poets
To celebrate their glorious deeds; I too possess that art,
And it is Ptolemy I must celebrate in my hymns—
For hymns are a reward even among the gods.
The woodman who enters Ida's* forest is overwhelmed by plenty,
And looks about him to see where he should begin his work.   10
What must I first describe among the countless gifts
Which the gods have showered on this supreme of kings?

By descent Ptolemy,* Lagus' son, received the skill to devise
And bring great plans to completion, beyond the imagination
Of other men. The Father* granted him equal honour with the
Immortal gods, and a golden throne stands for him in Zeus'
   house.
Next to him in friendship sits Alexander, scourge of the Persians,
The light glancing off his crown. Opposite, built of hard
   adamant,
Is the throne of Heracles, and there the centaur-killer feasts   20
With the other gods, pleased beyond measure at the fate of the
   sons
Of his sons,* because Zeus has relieved their limbs of the weight
Of old age, so that they, his descendants, are known as
   immortals;
Both these kings descend from the mighty son of Heracles, and
   both
Can trace their lineage to Heracles himself; who, when he has
   drunk his fill

Of sweet nectar, and goes from the feast to the house of his
  beloved wife,
Hands his bow and arm-slung quiver to one, and to the other
  gives   30
His iron club with its jagged knots; and they escort the bearded
  son of Zeus,
With his weapons, to white-ankled Hebe's fragrant chamber.

Famous Berenice,* too, surpassed all women of prudence, and
  brought
Joy to her parents, for Dione's* revered daughter, queen of
  Cyprus,
Had pressed her slender fingers on Berenice's fragrant breast.
Never, men say, has a wife so pleased her husband as she did
  Ptolemy;
He loved her, and yet was more loved in return. A man so
  blessed   40
May go in love to his dear wife's bed and in full confidence
Entrust his whole estate to their children. But the mind of a
Faithless wife is always straying towards other men—she gives
  birth easily,
But her children bear no likeness to their father. Aphrodite,
  loveliest
Of goddesses, you were Berenice's guardian. Through your
  agency
She did not pass over gloomy Acheron:* even before she
  reached
The ferryman of the dead and his sombre craft you stole her
  away
And set her in your temple, and shared your honours with
  her.*   50
She is kindly to all mortals, breathing into them gentle love,
And easing the pain of those who long for what they have lost.

Dark-browed lady of Argos,* you lay with Tydeus the
  Calydonian*
And bore him Diomedes,* killer of men. Deep-bosomed Thetis
  bore to
Peleus, the son of Aeacus, Achilles, hurler of the spear. Just so

Illustrious Berenice bore to soldier Ptolemy a soldier son, you,
    another
Ptolemy. When you were but a new-born child, first looking upon
    the
Light of day, the island Cos* took you from your mother and
    raised you;
There it was that Antigone's child, labouring in her birth-pangs,
Called upon Eilithyia who loosens women's girdles, and she stood
    close   60
In sympathy and gently poured painlessness over her limbs. This
    was the birth
Of an adored child, his father's image. When Cos saw him she
    shouted for joy,
And, holding the baby in her loving arms she spoke: 'Blessings on
    you, child;
May you bring to me the same honour which Phoebus Apollo
    bestowed on
Dark-crowned Delos. May you also bring honour to the hill of
    Triopia,*
And thus show equal favour to my Dorian neighbours; for lord
    Apollo
Loved Rhenaea* as much as he did Delos.' So the island spoke,
And high above it a mighty eagle shrieked three times in the
    clouds.   71
This is the bird of fate, and surely it was Zeus, Cronos' son, who
Sent the sign, Zeus who watches over revered kings, but chiefly
    those
He has loved from their moment of birth. Great wealth goes
    hand in hand
With such a man, and his rule spreads far abroad over land and
    sea.

There are numberless lands, peopled by numberless nations,
Who harvest their crops through the generosity of Zeus' rain,
But none is as fertile as low-lying Egypt when the overflowing Nile
Saturates and crumbles its soil; nor is any country so rich in
    towns   80
Of skilled inhabitants. Three hundred cities are established there;
Add to these thirty-three thousand, and after that twice three and

Three times nine—and princely Ptolemy is ruler of them all.

Beyond his borders he has carved off for himself tracts of Syria*

And of Phoenicia, and of Arabia too, and of Libya and the country of

The dark-skinned Ethiopians. His writ runs throughout Pamphylia,

And among the spear-throwers of Cilicia, and Lycia, and the martial men

Of Caria. He rules over the Cyclades, since the finest seafaring ships   90

Are his—indeed the world's entire sea and land and all its roaring

Rivers acknowledge Ptolemy's sway. He is surrounded by troops of

Horsemen and shield-bearing soldiers, armed in gleaming bronze.

In wealth he must outweigh all the kings of the world, so much

Flows each day into his sumptuous palace from every quarter.

His people go about their business in peace; no enemy on land can cross

The teeming Nile and raise their battle-cry in alien settlements, nor can

An armed invader leap from his swift ships to the sea-shore, to wreak   100

Havoc among the cattle herds of the Egyptians, while such a man as

Golden-haired Ptolemy the skilful spearman sits enthroned over these

Broad plains. His dearest wish, as befits a good king, is to keep his heritage

Safe and sound, and then by his efforts to make it grow. For all that,

The heaps of gold in his rich palace are not permitted to lie unused,

Like the treasure of industrious ants. Much is given to splendid temples

Of the gods, by way of first-fruits and benefactions. He is open-handed

To mighty kings, gives generously to cities and to his noble companions.   110

No singer proficient in the clear-voiced song at Dionysus' sacred
    contest*
Fails to receive the present which his art deserves, and Ptolemy's
Liberality is praised by the Muses' sacred speakers. What more
    splendid
Aim can a rich man pursue than to win a glorious reputation
    here on earth?
Even the sons of Atreus'* fame is secure, though the boundless
    wealth
They amassed at the sack of mighty Priam's palace is now lost,
    hidden
Somewhere in the misty darkness from which there is no return.

Unique among men both of former times and of today, whose
    footsteps   121
Leave their still-warm imprint in the trodden dust, Ptolemy has
    founded
Fragrant shrines to his beloved mother and to his father,* and has
    raised
Statues to them, gleaming with gold and ivory, to bring good
    fortune
To all men. Month after month, their altars grow red from the fat
    thighs
Of oxen, burnt by him and by his august wife. No finer woman
    ever
Embraced her husband in his palace, or gave such heartfelt love
To the man who is at once husband and brother. In the same
    way   131
Were the sacred marriages of the gods arranged, those whom
Queen Rhea bore to be rulers of Olympus; Zeus and Hera share
    one bed,
Prepared and purified by the scented hands of Iris,* still a virgin.

Farewell, lord Ptolemy. You shall be my hymn's theme no less
Than other demigods, and I believe my words will not be
    disregarded
By men to come; but as for excellence, you must pray to Zeus for
    that.

Idyll 18
The Marriage Song for Helen

Now, in Sparta once, in the palace of golden-haired Menelaus,
There were girls who wound fresh hyacinths into their hair, and
Stepped into the dance outside his freshly painted bridal room—
Twelve girls, from the city's foremost families, the great glory of
Sparta's youthful womanhood, at the time when Atreus' younger
    son,
Successful in his wooing, had locked the doors on them with his
Adored Helen, daughter of Tyndareus. So the girls sang in
    unison,
And moved their feet to the dance's complex measures,
While all the palace echoed to the sound of their wedding hymn:

'Asleep so soon, dear bridegroom?* So drowsy and so
Heavy-limbed? Or were you full of drink when your friends   10
Put you to bed? If you were so set on an early bedtime you
Should have left the girl with her doting mother,* to play with
Her friends and sleep till just before dawn. She'd still be your
    bride
Tomorrow, and the next day, and ever after for years to come.
Lucky bridegroom! Surely a good man's sneeze* escorted you
To Sparta, to compete against the other champions for your
Desire. Now only you among heroes can claim Zeus for a
Kinsman, since it is indeed a daughter of Zeus* who shares
Your bed, one unequalled among those who walk in Achaea.   20
What a wonderful thing it will be, if the child she bears resembles
Her mother! We her companions are all of an age with her,
And exercised with her by Eurotas'* washing-pools, oiling
    ourselves
Like men*—a company of girls two hundred and forty strong;
But none of us a match for peerless Helen. The face which
Dawn at its rising reveals is beautiful, O lady Night,

And beautiful is the vivid spring when winter loosens its grip;
So too did golden Helen's beauty shine in our company.
As a tall cypress rises above a garden or some rich ploughland   30
And graces it, or as a Thessalian horse is the glory of its chariot;
Just so is Helen's rosy skin the chief adornment of Sparta.
No woman spins a subtler thread and winds it from her basket
On to her spool, or, as she moves the shuttle at her inlaid loom,
Weaves and then shears a finer cloth from the long crossbar.
And again, no one is Helen's equal when she strikes music
From the lyre and sings a hymn to Artemis or to broad-breasted
Athene. Seductive charm has made its home in her eyes.

O lovely, graceful girl, you are now a wife, and the mistress   38
Of your house. As for us, early tomorrow we'll go to the
    flowering
Meadows where we race, to pick sweet-scented garlands, full of
Memories of you, as suckling lambs long for their mothers' teats.
We shall be the first to plait for you a wreath of ground-loving
Clover to hang on a shady plane-tree,* and we shall be the first
To make an offering of gleaming oil, dripped from our silver
    flasks,
Under that plane tree's shade. In its bark we shall cut these
    words, that
Passers-by may read its Dorian message: "Respect me; I am
    Helen's tree."

Farewell, bride—and farewell bridegroom, now joined to a noble
    house.
May these be your gifts: from fecund Leto,* delight in handsome
Children; from Cypris,* goddess Cypris, reciprocal love;   51
And from Zeus the son of Cronos, wealth which never fails,
And may it pass from one noble house to another. Sleep now,
Breast pillowed upon breast, while your breath mingles together
Love and desire. But do not forget to wake before the dawn;
For when day breaks, at the time when the cock first lifts
His handsome feathered neck to crow, we shall be here again.

O Hymen Hymenaeus,* show your favour to this marriage.'

Idyll 22
The Dioscuri

We hymn the twin sons of Leda and of Zeus, bearer
Of the aegis: Castor, and his brother Polydeuces—
A fearsome adversary to challenge to a boxing match,
When once he has strapped the oxhide thongs around his
    hands.
A second and a third time we hymn the twin sons of Thestius'
    child,*
Brothers from Lacedaemon, saviours of men* when their lives
Are poised on a knife-edge, and of horses caught in the
Bloody battle's panic. They rescue ships, which, having put to
    sea
In defiance of the stars that rise and set in the sky, run into
Perilous storms; at prow or stern, or wherever they will,   10
The winds heap up a huge mass of sea and hurl it into the
    vessel's
Hold. Both sides are smashed, the sails split apart, and
    shattered rigging
Hangs uselessly in the air. As night comes on, great sheets of
    rain
Fall from the sky; the wide sea crashes about them, hammered
    by
Blasts of stony hail. Even so, you heroes rescue them, hauling
    the
Ships up from the depths, crews and all—crews who believed
They were doomed to die. In an instant the winds drop, a sleek
    calm
Spreads over the open sea, and the clouds thin and disperse. 20
Out shine the Bears again, and dimly in between the Asses*
    the faint
Manger shows itself—a sure promise of fair sailing weather.

You both bring aid to mortal men, and so you both win their
  love;
You are horsemen, lyre-players, athletes, and singers of songs.
Which then shall be my song's first theme, Castor or
  Polydeuces?
My hymn is for both of you, but Polydeuces shall begin my
  song.*

Now, the Argo had escaped the clashing rocks and the
  unforgiving
Maw of snow-swept Pontus, and had come with its demigod
  crew
To the land of the Bebryces.* There the heroes rose from their
  benches   29
On both sides of the ship and disembarked by a single ladder
Down to a broad beach, a shore that was sheltered from the
  winds.
They made up their sleeping places, and busied themselves
  with
Lighting fires. But Castor the swift horseman and dark-skinned
Polydeuces drifted off alone, apart from their companions, and
Explored the wild and varied forest on the hill behind. There,
At the foot of a smooth cliff, they found an ever-flowing spring,
Brimming with pure water; in its depths pebbles gleamed, as if
Made of crystal or silver. Around it grew tall pines, poplars, 40
And plane trees, and leaf-crowned cypresses, and fragrant
  flowers,
Such as carpet meadows at the end of spring and summon
  hairy bees
To cheerful husbandry. There sat a giant of a man, taking his
  ease
In the sun. He was an awesome spectacle: his ears were
  thickened
By blows from leather mitts, and his huge chest and broad
  back swelled
Like the iron flesh of a hammered statue. Where his shoulders
  and hard arms
Met, the muscles jutted out like rounded boulders, polished
  smooth

By the whirling onrush of a winter torrent. A lion's skin, tied
  by its paws, 50
Hung from his neck and over his back. Polydeuces the
  champion spoke first:

POLYDEUCES Good day, stranger, whoever you are. What men
  own these lands?*

AMYCUS What's good about it, when all I see is men I have never
  seen before?

POLYDEUCES Don't distress yourself. We mean you no harm—and
  we're of good family.

AMYCUS Should I distress myself? You think I need you to tell me
  what to do?

POLYDEUCES You must be some wild kind of man; this is churlish
  and violent talk.

AMYCUS I am as you see me—but I'm not the one who is
  trespassing here.

POLYDEUCES Come with us, and we'll give you presents of
  friendship to bring back here. 60

AMYCUS Don't prattle to me about presents. I haven't got any
  presents for you.

POLYDEUCES Well! Won't you even give us permission to drink
  from this spring?

AMYCUS Just wait till your lips are parched with thirst, and then
  you'll find out.

POLYDEUCES Look—is it money you want, or what? How can we
  persuade you?

AMYCUS What I want is man-to-man combat. So put your fists up
  against mine.

POLYDEUCES Very well; just boxing, or leg-kicking and gouging
  eyes as well?

AMYCUS Boxing. So try your hardest, and call up whatever skill
  you have.

POLYDEUCES Fine. Who is it I'm to fight when I have bound my
  hands with leather?

AMYCUS He's here in front of you—and no weakling, either. Call
  him 'The Boxer'.

POLYDEUCES What about a prize? Have you anything here for us
  to fight for? 70

AMYCUS If you win, I shall be your slave, and if I win vice versa.
  That's the prize.

POLYDEUCES These rules suit a scrap between red-crested fighting
  cocks, not men.

AMYCUS We may prove to be fighting cocks, and we may turn out
  to be lions,

  But I'm not prepared for us to fight for any other prize.

So spoke Amycus, and picking up a hollow shell he blew a blast.

At the sound, the long-haired Bebryces came running up, and
  gathered

Under the plane trees' shade. Just so Castor, supreme in battle,
  went

To summon the heroes from their Thessalian ship.* When the
  two had

Strengthened their fists with oxhide thongs, and wound long
  leather   80

Straps around their arms, they squared up, breathing
  murderous intent

At one another. Then a hard struggle began, as each man tried
  his utmost

To seize the place where the sun would shine from behind his
  back.

It was your guile, Polydeuces, which fooled your hulking
  opponent,

So that Amycus' eyes were dazzled by the full force of the sun.

Anger rose in his heart and he lunged forward, his fists flailing.

As he charged ahead the son of Tyndareus* caught him on the
  point

Of his chin. Enraged, Amycus bore in with lowered head,
  aiming

To turn the fight into a mêlée. The Bebryces cheered, and on
  the other side   90

The heroes urged on strong Polydeuces, afraid that in the
  narrow

Space this Tityos-like monster* might bring his weight to bear
  and so

Overwhelm their man. But the son of Zeus shifted from side to
  side,

Cutting Amycus repeatedly with jabs from both his fists, and so
    held up

The charge of Poseidon's son, for all his brute strength. He was

Rooted to the ground, drunk with punches and spitting out
    blood.

A loud cheer rose from the heroes, when they saw the ugly
    wounds

Around Amycus' mouth and jaw, and his eyes narrowed to slits
    in his   100

Swollen face. Lord Polydeuces drove him mad, throwing feints
    from

Every side, and when he saw the man was at his mercy he
    landed a

Downward blow on his forehead, above the nose, skinning his
    brow

Down to the bone. Back Amycus fell, stretching his length on a
    carpet of flowers;

But soon he was back on his feet, and the savage bout was
    renewed,

Each seeking to batter the other to death with the hard leather.

The chief of the Bebryces swung punches at his opponent's
    chest,   110

And below his neck, while invincible Polydeuces jabbed
    without pause

At Amycus' face, smashing it with his fists into a dreadful pulp.

His sweating flesh collapsed, and his colossal form shrank in on
    itself,

While Polydeuces' limbs enlarged, and his skin shone in the
    heat of the fight.

How then did the son of Zeus deliver the *coup de grace* to this
    huge

Mound of a man? Tell me, goddess, for you know; and I your
    interpreter

To other men shall make your meaning clear as it most pleases
    you.

Amycus now looked for a knockout blow. He stood up on his
    guard,

Leant obliquely across Polydeuces, and grasped his left hand
In his own left; then, shifting his weight to the right, he swung
    an   120
Uppercut from the hip with his great broad fist. Had the blow
    landed
It would have maimed the king of Amyclae,* but he ducked
    aside, and,
Punching straight from the shoulder, hammered Amycus
    below his
Left temple. The bone cracked open, and the dark blood
    spurted out
In a rush. With his left, Polydeuces smashed into his mouth,
    rattling
The close-set teeth. A rain of rapid blows ravaged Amycus'
    face,
Until his cheeks were reduced to pulp. He collapsed,
    measuring his
Length on the ground, his mind clouded, and held out both his
    hands
In surrender, for he was near to death. Though you were the
    victor,   130
Boxer Polydeuces, you did no further violence to Amycus;
    instead
He swore you a great oath, calling upon his father Poseidon,
    the god
Of the sea, that he would never again maltreat strangers
    unprovoked.

This, then, is my hymn for you, my lord Polydeuces. It is now
    time
To sing of Castor, son of Tyndareus: driver of swift horses,
Fighter with the spear, armoured with the brazen breastplate.

The two sons of Zeus had abducted and were carrying off the
    two
Daughters of Leucippus.* Giving chase in hot pursuit were two
    brothers,
Lynceus and the mighty Idas, sons of Aphareus, who was now
    dead;

They had thought they were to be bridegrooms. All four had
   reached the   140
Tomb of Aphareus, and there they leaped from their chariots,
   carrying
Their heavy spears and curved shields, and rushed at each
   other.
Lynceus was the first to speak, shouting aloud from under his
   helmet:
'Gentlemen! Why these naked swords? Why this desire for a
   fight?
Why pick a quarrel over other men's brides? *We* were
   promised these
Girls by Leucippus long ago, and his oath named us as
   bridegrooms.
You do wrong to covet other men's brides, beguiling the girls'
   father
With oxen and mules and other gifts, and cheating us of our
   marriage.   150
I am not a man of many words, but I have told you time and
   again,
Both of you, face to face: "My friends, it cannot be right for a
   hero
To seek a bride in this way, when she is already betrothed.
   Surely
Sparta is large enough, and Elis,* breeder of horses—and then
   there is
Arcadia rich in sheep, and Achaea's cities, Messene and Argos,
   and
The whole coastline of Sisyphus. Girls by the thousand live
   there,
Raised in their fathers' houses, and every one of them clever
   and   160
Beautiful. You could have your pick of these for a bride; every
   father
Wants his daughter to marry a man of good birth, and you are
   the cream
Of heroes, you and your fathers, and all the bloodline of your
   forbears.

My friends, leave us to make the marriages we have planned, and

Let us together see how we can find some other brides for you."

That is the kind of speech I have made, many times, but the

Wind's breath has carried my words away to the waves of the sea,

And my words have not found favour. You are stiff and stubborn—

We are cousins from our father, so be persuaded, even at this late hour.'   170

[*The beginning of Castor's reply is lost from the manuscripts.*]*

'. . . But if your hearts are set on a fight, and we must allow this grim

Quarrel to erupt into spears' bloodletting, then let Idas and my brother,

Strong Polydeuces, draw back and keep their hands out of the battle.

Lynceus and I, the younger pair, will submit to Ares' judgement,

And thus spare our fathers complete grief. One death in each house

Will be enough; those who are left can welcome their friends to their

Weddings with these girls, as bridegrooms and not as corpses. That is

A small price to pay, and the just way, to conclude great enmity.'   180

So he spoke, and the god did not intend his words to go unfulfilled.

The older brothers took off their armour and laid it on the ground.

Lynceus strode forward, waving his strong spear below his shield's

Outer rim, and just so Castor brandished his twin weapons; above

Each helmet nodded a horsehair plume. At first they fought
   with spears,
Jabbing at their opponent whenever they saw a patch of naked
   skin;
But before either could inflict a wound their spears stuck fast
In the other's dreadful shield, and were shattered. So then they
   drew   190
Swords from sheaths, and pressed on with the murderous work,
Without respite. Time and again Castor battered Lynceus'
   broad shield
And horsehair-crested helmet, while keen-eyed Lynceus
   matched him,
Stabbing at his shield and almost shearing off his crimson
   crest.
Then Lynceus swung with his sharp sword at Castor's left
   knee,
But the other sprang backwards, and sliced his fingers off.
   Wounded,
Lynceus dropped his sword, and quickly turned to run to his
Father's tomb, where mighty Idas lay, watching the cousins
   fight.   200
But Tyndareus' son was at his heels, and thrust his broad
   sword
Into his side and out again through the navel, and the bronze
   blade
Split the guts inside him. Lynceus' head dropped, he sank
   down,
And a heavy sleep swam down over his eyes. Nor was
   Laocoosa
To see her other son happily married at his father's hearth.
Messenian Idas had torn up his father's tombstone and was
   making to
Hurl it at his brother's killer; but Zeus protected Castor, and
   struck the   210
Carved stone from his hands, and his fiery bolt reduced him to
   ashes.
It is no small thing to go to war with the sons of Tyndareus;
   they are

Powerful in their own right, and sons of a powerful father.

Farewell, sons of Leda; may you always bring my hymns respect

And honour. All singers are dear to the sons of Tyndareus, to Helen,

And to the heroes who answered Menelaus' call and plundered Troy.

It was the singer of Chios* who brought you fame, my lords, when he

Sang of Priam's city, and of the Achaean ships; of the battles round

Troy, and of Achilles, that tower in war. I, in my turn, bring you   220

Honeyed songs of the clear-voiced Muses; some they give me, and

Some come from my store. Songs are prized by the gods above all things.

Idyll 24
The Childhood of Heracles

Once, when Heracles was ten months old, Alcmena of Midea*
Bathed him and Iphicles* his brother, younger than Heracles by a
Night, gave them their fill of milk, and put them down to sleep
On a bronze shield*—fine armour which Amphitryon had
    stripped from
Pterelaus* after he had killed him. Stroking her sons' heads she
    murmured:
'Sleep sweetly, my babies, and wake restored; sleep without cares,
Brothers, my children, my life. Blessed be your rest, and blessed
    your
Dawn awakening.' As she spoke she rocked the great shield, and
    sleep   10
Received them. But at the time when the Bear at midnight dips
    to its rest,
Next to Orion's mighty shining shoulder, cunning Hera
    despatched
Two terrible, monstrous serpents with arching dark blue coils
Towards the broad threshold where the palace's latticed
    doorposts
Stood, with strict instructions to devour the infant Heracles. They
Twisted and writhed their way over the ground on bloodthirsty
    bellies,
Evil fire flashed from their eyes, and their jaws spat lethal poison.
But when they were close to touching the boys with their
    flickering   20
Tongues, Alcmena's sons awoke—for Zeus sees everything—and
The house was flooded with light. When Iphicles saw the evil
    snakes
Rearing above the hollow shield with their cruel teeth he let out a
    scream,

And kicked the woollen blanket off his legs, in a frenzy to get
    away.

But Heracles stood his ground, and shot out his hands and
    clamped them

Fast in a crushing grip, tight on the creatures' throats, at the
    point where

Deadly snakes keep their vile venom, which even the gods
    abominate.

At this they wrapped their coils around the child, this infant, still
    at his   30

Mother's breast (though never one to weep); they clenched their
    spines,

Then let them go limp, in agonized attempts to break from his

Tenacious grasp. Alcmena first heard the scream, and woke with
    a start:

'Amphitryon, get up! I'm dreadfully scared! Get up—don't
    wait

To put your sandals on. Did you not hear those loud screams—
    it's our

Younger boy. And look: it's deep midnight, but we can see the
    walls

As clearly as if it was bright dawn. Dear husband, there is
    something

Wrong in the house—there must be.' So she spoke, and
    Amphitryon   40

Did as she said and got out of the bed . He seized his decorated
    sword,

Which hung as always from a peg above the cedar bed. As he
    reached

For his newly-plaited belt, and with his other hand pulled down
    his

Great scabbard of lotus wood, the spacious room grew dark
    again.

At this he called to his slaves, who were snoring in heavy sleep:

'Quick, get light from the hearth and bring it here! Shove the
    great

Bars back from the doors!' A Phoenician slave-woman,* who
    slept

In the place where the corn was ground, shouted: 'Stout-hearted
    slaves,
Get up! It's the master who is calling you!' So the slaves lit their
    lamps 50
And came at a run, and the palace was filled with people bustling
    about.
When they saw the infant Heracles holding the snakes in his soft
    hands
With a vice-like grip, they cried out in amazement. But the boy
Held the creatures up for his father to see, and danced with
    childish joy
At what he had done; he laughed, and laid the dreadful monsters,
Sluggish with the sleep of death, at Amphitryon's feet. Iphicles
    was
Stiff with fear and hysterical, and Alcmena hugged him to her
    breast; 60
But Amphitryon put Heracles to rest again under his lambswool
Blanket, and returning to his own bed composed himself for
    sleep.

As soon as the cocks' third crow had announced the break of day
Alcmena summoned Teiresias,* the unerring prophet of truth.
    To him
She told the story of this strange phenomenon, and asked him to
    explain
The meaning. 'And if the gods have some unpleasantness in store
For us, do not hide it from me, simply out of respect. We all
Know that mortals cannot escape the destiny which fate's distaff
Directs at them. But then, son of Eueres, you are a prophet, and I
    only 71
Tell you what you already know.' That is what the queen said,
    and
Teiresias replied: 'Be reassured, lady, mother of noble children,
    Perseus'
Grandchild, be reassured. Store in your heart the best of what is
    to come.
By the dear light of my eyes that vanished long ago, I say this to
    you:
Many Achaean women will name Alcmena in their songs, when,

Late in the evening, they rub the soft yarn across their knees. You will be

Honoured too among Argive women, because a great man will climb

To the starry heaven; I mean this son of yours, destined to be a broad-chested   80

Hero, stronger than all beasts and all other men. It is ordained that he will

Carry out twelve labours and after that will live in the house of Zeus,

Though a funeral pyre in Trachis* will consume his mortal part. By his

Marriage he will be called a son of the gods,* the same immortals who

Sent these monsters to devour your son by stealth. So now, lady,

You must make sure there is fire beneath these ashes; then you should

Collect dry sticks of bramble, camelthorn or paliurus, or parched and   90

Wind-seared pearwood, and on this wild firewood you must burn these

Snakes, at midnight, the hour when they sought to kill your child.

At dawn a slave girl must collect the fire's ashes, and take them

Over the river to the jagged cliffs beyond our country's borders, and

Throw them away, every single scrap; then she should return without

A backward glance.* *Your* first task is to fumigate the palace with

Pure sulphur, and then to take a branch bound with wool and sprinkle

Everything with clean water mixed with salt, according to custom.

Lastly, sacrifice a boar to Zeus the Lord, that you may ever after lord it   100

Over your enemies.' Teiresias spoke, and leaving his seat of ivory he

Went on his way, though he carried the burden of many years.

Heracles grew, nursed by his mother, like a young tree in an
  orchard,
And was known as the son of Amphitryon of Argos. He learnt his
  letters
From the old hero Linus,* son of Apollo, a guardian who never
  slept.
Eurytus* taught him to bend his bow and to shoot an arrow at
  the mark;
He was a wealthy man, who had inherited broad lands from his
  father.
Eumolpus,* Philammon's son, shaped the boy's hands round the
  boxwood lyre,   110
And taught him the singer's art. As for the tricks which Argive
  wrestlers use,
Swinging their hips to trip and throw each other, and all the
  stratagems which
Boxers skilled with the leather thongs employ, and ruses invented
  by
All-in fighters to develop the art of grappling on the ground—all
  these
Heracles learnt from Harpalycus* of Panopeus, Hermes' son. No
  one about
To fight this man in a contest could look upon him with
  equanimity, even
From a safe distance, so threatening was the brow which jutted
  over his
Grim face. But the art of driving chariot horses, and how to
  round the
Turning-post in safety, and not to graze the wheel's hub,
  Amphitryon   120
Taught his son with loving care; he himself had won many a
  prize in the
Swift races at Argos, nurturer of horses, and the chariots he had
  driven
Had survived intact, except that time had ruined their leather
  reins.
How to crouch behind his shield with spear at the ready, how to
  lunge at

His opponent and to withstand the sword's onslaught, how to
    draw up
A squadron of men, to estimate the strength of an enemy troop as
    it
Advances, how to command cavalry—all this he learnt from
    Castor,*
Hippalus' son; he was an exile from Argos, because Adrastus had
    given
His whole estate and broad vineyards there to Tydeus,* who was
    living   130
On them then in that horse-rearing land. No demigod could
    match Castor
As a soldier, not until old age had worn away the edge of his
    youth.

This then was the schooling devised for Heracles by his loving
    mother.
For his bed he had a lion-skin, spread next to his father, which
He greatly enjoyed. His supper was roast meat, and an enormous
Dorian loaf in a basket, enough to fill a country labourer's belly;
    but
In the day he ate little, and nothing that was cooked. He wore a
Simple tunic, which reached to just below his knees . . .   140

[*Here the manuscript breaks off*]

Idyll 26
The Bacchantes

There were three sisters: Ino, Autonoe, and white-cheeked
    Agave,
And they led three companies up to the mountain. There they
    cut leaves
From the dense growth of the wild oak, and living ivy and
    creeping
Asphodel, and in a sacred open field they built twelve altars:
    three for Semele,*
And nine for Dionysus. From a chest they lifted out the sacred
    offerings
They had shaped, and in holy silence laid them on the new-built
    altars,
Just as the god had taught them; for this was Dionysus' pleasure.
But Pentheus was watching all their preparations, from a high
    rock;   10
He was hidden in an ancient mastich bush which grew nearby.
The first to catch sight of him was Autonoe; she gave a dreadful
    cry,
Dashed to the altars, and with a kick scattered the sacred objects
Of the god of frenzy, upon which the profane may not look.
Madness possessed her, and madness quickly entered the others.
Pentheus, terrified, tried to escape, while they drew their dresses
Up through their belts as far as their thighs and set off in pursuit.
'What do you want with me, you women?' shouted Pentheus.
Autonoe replied, 'You will know soon enough, before I answer
    you'.   19
At this his mother, roaring like a lioness over her cubs, tore off
    her
Son's head. Ino planted her foot on his stomach and wrenched
    one

Mighty shoulder clean away, shoulder-blade and all, while Autonoe
Tore away the other. All that was left of his flesh was parcelled out
Among the other women, and they all returned to Thebes splashed
With blood, bringing not Pentheus but mourning* down from the mountain.

Why should I care?* The enemies of Dionysus matter to no one, not even
Those who suffer a worse death than Pentheus, not even if they are
Children of nine or ten. What *I* pray for is a pure life, and to be acceptable   30
To those who are pure. On such terms is the eagle honoured by Zeus the
Aegis-bearer. The children of the pious, not the impious, live the better life.

Farewell then, Dionysus, set down on snowy Dracanus* by lofty Zeus
When he had unstitched his huge thigh.* Farewell, too, lovely Semele
And her sisters, ladies of Cadmus' city* honoured by many a noble woman.
It was Dionysus' urging that impelled you to this deed, and it bears no blame.
Let no man raise his voice in reproach at the actions of the gods.

Idyll 28
The Distaff

Distaff, the wool-spinner's friend, gift of grey-eyed Athene to
    women
Skilled in the housewife's craft: come cheerfully with me to
    Neileus'*
Glorious city, where pliant reeds grow green in the temple
    precinct
Of Cypris.* We shall ask Zeus for a fair wind on our voyage, so
    that
I may feast my eyes on the sight of my dear friend Nicias,* sacred
    son
Of the sweet-voiced Graces, and be warmed by his welcome in
    return.
There I shall place you, my gift of finely crafted ivory, in the
    hands
Of Nicias' wife. With her you will spin quantities of fine yarn   10
For men's clothes, and also for the gauzy stuffs that women wear.
For ewes in their pastures could be shorn of their soft fleeces
Twice in each year, and Theugenis* of the pretty ankles would
    not
Slacken her work—so industrious she is, and so prudent in her
    ways.
Distaff, I would not send you to a lazy or neglectful woman's
    house,
For you come from *my* land, from the town that was founded
By Archias* of Ephyra long ago: the very essence of the isle of
    Sicily,
A city of famous men. But now you must go to the house of a   19
Man who is deeply skilled in the use of drugs which protect men
From deadly maladies, to live among the Ionian folk of lovely
    Miletus.

Your task is to bring Theugenis fame for her distaff among the
Women of her city, and to remind her for ever of her poet-friend.
When people see you they will say: 'In truth, great affection lies
In a little present, and every gift from a friend is to be treasured.'

Idyll 29
To a Boy

In vino veritas,* dear lad, as the saying goes; I am in my cups,
So I too must speak the truth. I shall tell you my inmost thoughts:
You will never love me with all your heart. I know this is true;
Your beauty gives meaning to half my life, while the other half is
Nothing. When you are good to me, I spend my day among the
    blessed,
But when you are not I'm plunged in darkness. Is this fair, to
    make   9
Your lover miserable? You are young, so listen to an older man;
When you see the benefit of my advice, you will thank me.
Keep to a single tree, and make one nest in it, where no wild
Creeping thing can reach you. You perch on one branch today,
And another tomorrow, always looking for the next place to
    lodge.
If someone sees your handsome face and praises it, you make him
There and then a lifelong friend, while you treat your first lover
    as   20
Yesterday's man. You have grown too arrogant; the best rule is to
Stick to your own kind. This is the way to win respect in the
    town,
And moreover Love will treat you well—Love, which crushes
Men's hearts with ease, and has enfeebled even my iron will.
I beg you, by your soft mouth, to remember that one year ago
You were younger. Wrinkled old age creeps up on us more
    quickly
Than we can spit, and youth wears wings upon its shoulders—
Once lost, it cannot be recalled. We are not quick enough to
    capture   30
Things that fly. Consider this, be good to me, and love me
    equally,

Without guile. Then, when your cheeks begin to show the beard
Of manhood, we can be friends, as Achilles was to Patroclus*.
But if you cast my words to the winds, and say in your heart
'Stop! Why must you keep pestering me?', though now I'd go
And fetch you the golden apples,* or bring back Cerberus,* guardian
Of the dead, that would mean an end to my painful passion; I'd not
Come to my house door to see you, even if you summoned me.   39

Idyll 30
To Another Boy

Oh, the agony of this cursed sickness! It's two months now that
This recurring fever has held me in its grip: a passion for a boy—
Not all that beautiful, but he exudes charm from top to toe, and a
Sweet smile touches his cheek. Some days the virus holds me fast,
Some days it leaves me alone, but the time will soon come when
There will be no respite, not even the comfort of sleep; for
    yesterday
As he passed me, too shy to look me in the eye he glanced at me
Quickly, with head lowered, and blushed. At this Love tightened
    its hold
On my heart, and I returned home nursing a fresh wound in my
    breast.   10
So then I summoned up my heart, and addressed myself at
    length:
'Not again! What *are* you doing? Is there no end to your idiocy?
You should remember that the hair on your head is white, and
    it's
High time to learn some sense. Your youthful looks have gone;
    don't
Behave as if you were tasting the pleasures of life for the first
    time.
You forget, too, that older men are well advised to keep
    themselves
From falling in love with boys, because it brings with it such pain.
To boys, their lives seem to speed along, as if borne on the hooves
Of a swift deer; tomorrow they can always alter their sails and
Embark on a different course. Furthermore, the prime of their
Sweet manhood is spent with those of their own age. But the
    lover   20
Lives on memories, and longing devours him to the very bones;

His nights are constantly disturbed by dreams, and a whole year
Will not suffice to rid him of his painful malady.' These, and many
Like them, were the grievances I put before my heart, but it replied:
'If you believe you can master ingenious Love, you must also believe
That counting the myriad stars above our heads is an easy task.
That is why now, whether I like it or not, I must stretch out my neck
And strain against the yoke. Such, my friend, is the will of the god who
Deceived even the powerful mind of Zeus, and the lady of Cyprus herself.   30
With one breath he lifts me up and quickly whisks me away, like a
Leaf that is stirred by light winds and lives only for a day.'

Explanatory Notes

IDYLL I

This poem, with its beautiful, musical opening, injunction to 'begin bucolic song', and account of the 'sufferings of Daphnis', the first bucolic singer and/or original subject of bucolic song, seems always to have been placed first in ancient collections of Theocritus' poetry, and came to symbolize the essence of the bucolic genre; cf. above, p. xvi on the description of the marvellous cup. The use of refrains in Thyrsis' song points to traditions of popular song, and the mysterious allusiveness of the account of Daphnis' suffering and fate similarly suggests that this is a founding 'myth' handed down by generations of rustics. Thus does Theocritus ground his new literary creation in the practices of the people and suggest the timelessness of its origins.

There is no explicit setting, but Thyrsis is from Etna and sings a Sicilian song.

2 *pipe*: the *syrinx*, 'Pan pipes', was made of reeds cut to equal lengths and bound together by wax; differential pitch was created by stopping each reed with wax at different points. Only later did an instrument composed of reeds of descending length become normal.

3 *Pan*: half-man and half goat, Pan (the origin of 'panic', the supernatural terror which this god can cause) was the divine pipe-player who haunted mountains and remote fields and ensured the fertility and safety of flocks. He also had a prodigious sexual appetite (particularly for nymphs).

19 *Daphnis*: the legendary first bucolic singer, and also the subject of bucolic song *par excellence*, cf. above p. xvi. He is usually said to have been a Sicilian cowherd who was loved by a nymph who warned him that if he slept with any other woman he would lose his sight; an infatuated princess made him drunk and slept with him, thus bringing the predicted punishment down on Daphnis. In the mysteriously allusive song which Thyrsis proceeds to sing, Daphnis

appears to hold out, like Hippolytus, against the power of *eros*, though the reason for his resistance is unclear.

21 *Priapus*: an ithyphallic deity whose cult spread from Lampsacus in the Hellespont all over the Greek world. Priapus is closely associated with Dionysus and, like Pan, is a fertility god with special responsibility for crops and fruit. His erect penis is a permanent reminder of the power of the sexual drive which Daphnis will try to resist.

26 *a deep cup*: the description ('*ekphrasis*') which follows marks out the space of Theocritus' poetry against the scenes of war and peace on Achilles' divinely-made shield in *Iliad* 18. The envisaged arrangement of the figures is unclear, but it seems likely that all are carved in relief on the outside of the bowl, 'inside' (31) the ivy bower.

57 *Calydnos*: the modern Kalimno, an island lying off the NW coast of Cos.

64 The refrains which punctuate Thyrsis' song connect it with traditions of popular, oral song, in keeping with the imagined milieu of bucolic song, and with laments; the latter are obviously appropriate to the subject of the song.

65 *Etna*: not merely the great mountain in E. Sicily, but also the name of a town at its foot.

66 Cf. Milton, *Lycidas* 50 ff; 'Where were ye, Nymphs, when the remorseless deep | Closed o'er the head of your loved Lycidas? | For neither were ye playing on the steep | Where your old bards, the famous Druids, lie | Nor on the shaggy top of Mona high, | Nor yet where Deva spreads her wizard stream.'

67 *Peneus*: a river of northern Greece which flows through the valley of Tempe.

67 *Pindus*: a mountain range in northern Greece dividing Thessaly from Epirus.

68 *Anapus*: a river flowing into the sea near Syracuse.

69 *Acis*: another river of E. Sicily; cf. Ovid, *Met.* 13. 870–97.

71 The 'pathetic fallacy' in which nature responds to events in the human world was to become one of the most important figures of pastoral poetry.

77 *Hermes*: one of this god's prominent functions was as a protector of

flocks, like his son Pan. Some later sources make Hermes Daphnis' father.

95   *Cypris*: 'the lady of Cyprus', i.e. Aphrodite.

106   *Anchises*: the cowherd of Mt. Ida (near Troy) for whom Aphrodite conceived a passion and to whom she bore Aeneas, cf. the *Homeric Hymn to Aphrodite*. The affair was a cause of great shame to the goddess.

109   *Adonis*: a young shepherd, beloved by Aphrodite, who was killed by a wild boar, but allowed to return each year to spend some time with the goddess, cf. Idyll 15, Bion's *Lament for Adonis*.

112   *Diomedes*: the Greek hero who wounded Aphrodite in the fighting at Troy (*Iliad* 5. 335–430).

117   *Arethusa*: a famous spring in Syracuse.

118   *Thybris*: perhaps a rocky gorge above Syracuse (Monte Crimiti), but identification is uncertain.

123   *Lycaeus*: a mountain range in SW Arcadia, with a famous sanctuary of Pan.

124   *Maenalus*: another Arcadian mountain connected with Pan.

125   *peak of Helice*: probably a circumlocution for Mt. Lycaeus; Helice was identified with Callisto, the daughter of the eponymous Arcadian hero, Lycaon.

126   *son of Lycaon*: probably Maenalus, but Theocritus' learned geography remains somewhat obscure for us.

140   *came to the river*: Daphnis' end is designedly mysterious: is this just the river of the Underworld, or did Daphnis drown (? commit suicide) in a pool connected with his love?

148   *Aegilus*: the hero of the Attic deme Aegilia, mentioned elsewhere as producing excellent figs.

150   *the Hours*: daughters of Zeus and Themis who bestow beauty and fruitfulness.

IDYLL 2

A remarkable first-person narrative by Simaetha, who has been abandoned by her lover Delphis and who resorts to love-magic to win him back and/or punish him (the confusion is a natural one). For the debt to the mimes of Sophron cf. above, p. xix; the abuse of the slave in the opening section of the poem is very typical of the mime. The essential ordinariness of the events is set off by evocations of epic heroines (the abandoned Ariadne, etc.) and echoes of higher literature (Homer, Sappho), but the irony with which the naive Simaetha is depicted does not conceal the seriousness and sadness with which she seeks to come to terms with her fate. Striking parallels with extant magical papyri show how this poem raises popular traditions to the level of high art.

The setting is unclear, though many have thought Cos likely (cf. below on 'Philinus').

For illustration and discussion of ancient magical practices cf. H. Betz, *The Greek Magical Papyri in translation* (Chicago, 1986), G. Luck, *Arcana Mundi* (Baltimore, 1985), F. Graf, *Magic in the Ancient World* (Cambridge, Mass., 1997), J. J. Winkler, *The Constraints of Desire* (London, 1990).

1   *bay leaves*: probably (despite v. 23) used, like the red wool of v. 2, to protect the performer against the powerful effects of his/her own magic.

3   *bind*: the standard term (in Greek *katadeo*) for 'putting a spell' on someone; such 'binding spells' are *katadesmoi*.

12 *Hecate*: a goddess of magic and dark powers; dogs were sacrificed to her, and barking may signal her approach (cf. 30–1).

15 *Circe*: the famous enchantress of the *Odyssey* whose magic turned Odysseus' men into pigs.

16 *Medea*: Circe's niece, most celebrated in antiquity from Euripides' tragedy about her punishment of Jason's faithlessness by the killing of their children; cf. also Pindar, *Pythian* 4. Her magical powers had allowed Jason and the Argonauts to bring the Golden Fleece back to Greece and had rejuvenated Jason's father by boiling him with magic herbs.

16 *Perimede*: Perhaps an inaccurate memory of 'Agamede of the golden hair' whose knowledge of magical drugs is celebrated in Homer (*Iliad* 11. 740–1); the name suggests 'more Medea than Medea'.

17 *Magic wheel . . .*: the refrain suggests both the repetitive, hypnotic effect of 'binding' magic (cf. Aeschylus, *Eumenides* 321–96) and the popular character of Simaetha's magic. The 'magic wheel', lit. *iunx*, was a circular disc which, when rotated quickly, emitted a whining sound to bewitch the beloved. Some texts combine this wheel with a bird, also called *iunx*, which was also used in magic,

cf. S. I. Johnson, *Transactions of the American Philological Society*, 125 (1995), 177–206.

28 *Artemis*: Hecate (n. above) and Artemis, the great goddess of hunting and the wild, are often identified in the post-classical period.

31 *the bronze gong*: a loud metallic noise is used to guard against the evil powers which the magician him/herself has aroused.

39 *Myndus*: a Carian sea-town.

40 *whirler of bronze*: a 'bullroarer' which emits a rising moan as it is whirled ever faster; similar objects are familiar in the cult and magical practices of many cultures.

46 Theseus' abandonment on Dia (Naxos) of Ariadne, the Cretan princess who had saved him in the Minotaur's labyrinth, is normally ascribed to forgetfulness, though the causes of that forgetfulness are very variously explained.

51 *sleek wrestling school*: 'sleek' because the young athletes treated their bodies with olive-oil.

58 *lizard . . . poison drink*: probably as a love-philtre rather than a destructive poison, but Simaetha's magic as a whole wavers (with psychological truth?) between attempts to recover and to destroy Delphis.

66 *a basket-bearer*: an important female role in many Greek cults.

69 *Learn, lady Moon . . .*: the narrative too has a refrain, not just because Simaetha's instructions are currently being carried out, but also because the telling of this tale of (as Simaetha sees it) injustice ought to rouse dark powers against Delphis.

82 *One look, and I was mad*: Simaetha echoes the description of Zeus' overpowering desire for Hera at *Iliad* 14. 293–4 (a passage echoed also at Idyll 3. 42); the contrast between the situations creates a complex effect of pathos and irony.

88 *Zantean dye*: a yellowish dye produced from the wood of a shrub ('fustic').

106 *colder than snow . . .*: Simaetha now echoes Sappho's famous description of the symptoms of erotic passion (Sappho fr. 31, translated by Catullus in Poem 51); once again (cf. n. above) we are invited to compare her experience with that of characters from high literature. 'Stiff as a doll's', however, is an image drawn from a much more humble world.

112 *fixed his faithless eyes on the ground*: a gesture associated with the epic
     Odysseus (cf. *Iliad* 3. 217) prepares for the plausible smooth-talking
     which is to follow.

116 *Philinus*: the name is very common and suggestive of *philein*, 'to
     love/kiss' (cf. the description 'graceful'), but there was in fact a
     very successful Coan athlete called Philinus in the first half of the
     third century.

120 *Dionysus' apples*: Dionysus can be a god of vegetation generally, as
     well as specifically of the vine, but the particular point here is
     obscure; Delphis imagines himself coming to Simaetha's house on
     a *komos* (cf. n. to p. 91), and such revelry took place under the sign
     of Dionysus, god of wine. Apples are perhaps the most common
     love-token in Greek poetry and magic.

121 *Heracles' holy garland*: Heracles is said to have introduced the white
     poplar to Greece.

130 *Cypris*: cf. n. on p. 87.

133 *Hephaestus kindles on Lipara*: the forge of Hephaestus, the god of fire
     and metal-working, was often located on one of the Aeolian
     islands (usually Lipara or Hiera (modern Vulcano)) near Sicily.

152 *unmixed wine*: Greeks normally diluted their wine with water, and
     undiluted wine was used only for special toasts, such as here to the
     beloved, or by the scandalously drunken.

154 *garlands*: the komast (cf. n. to p. 91) left garlands at his beloved's
     door as a token of his devotion.

162 *Assyrian stranger*: the East was regarded by Greeks as the home of
     dangerous, magical arts; the anonymity increases the mysterious
     menace.

IDYLL 3

This poem transfers to the countryside a familiar scenario of urban
poetry in which a man, often accompanied by friends and somewhat the
worse for drink, tries to secure admittance to his beloved's house by
singing in the street outside. In this case the helpless lover is a goatherd
aping the courting customs of the literate, though he presumably could,
if he so wished, simply walk into his beloved's cave; he is not 'locked out'
in any real sense. In its pauses and probable refocusing of scene after the
opening address to Tityrus, there is a clear relation to traditions of

comedy and semi-dramatic performance, and we hear of solo per-
formers called *magodoi*, whose repertoire included acting the part of 'a
drunk man going on a revel to his mistress', and whose performances
often borrowed from comedy (Athenaeus 14. 621c–d). Idyll 3 may be
seen as a very sophisticated 'literary' version of such a script.

There is no clear indication of setting.

1 *to serenade*: lit. 'go on a *komos*'.

1 *Amaryllis*: the name means something like 'Miss Sparkle'.

7 *your cave*: it is not perhaps impossible that unattached women
sometimes took up residence in, or conducted business from,
caves, but it is more likely that the goatherd is obsessed with a
nymph whom he may merely have fantasized.

10 *apples*: cf. n. to p. 90, *Dionysus' apples*.

16 *suckled by a lioness*: the lion's savagery is imagined to pass to its
young through the milk. For the poetic figure cf. *Iliad* 16. 34–5
(Patroclus to Achilles) 'the grey sea and the sheer cliffs bore you, so
unbending is your mind'.

29 *the love-in-absence*: an obscure reference to a kind of 'she loves me—
she loves me not' game, where the answer seems to have depended
on whether a particular leaf stuck to the skin when it was smacked
down on the arm.

31 *tells fortunes with a sieve*: perhaps by sieving beans or gravel and
'reading' the pattern formed on the ground.

39 The goatherd's song, a 'paraklausithyron' or 'song in front of a
locked door', attempts a seriousness of poetic level and subject-
matter quite different from what has preceded. He seeks to win
over Amaryllis with mythological instances of 'pastoral' love, but
the effect is bathetic at best.

41 Atalanta would only marry a man who could beat her in a
running-race; this Hippomenes achieved by dropping golden
apples, which he had received from (in various versions)
Aphrodite, Dionysus, or the Garden of the Hesperides, at various
stages of the race.

42 *in that instant . . . was mad*: cf. note on 2. 82.

43 Melampus brought cattle back from northern Greece—Othrys is
a mountain range in Thessaly—to the Peloponnese so that his
brother Bias could marry Pero, whose father had demanded the

return of the cattle. Pero later bore Alphesiboea ('she who brings cattle'). This represents for the goatherd another glorious 'bucolic' act in the service of love.

46 *Adonis*: cf. n. on p. 87.

46 *Cytherea*: 'lady of Cythera', i.e. Aphrodite.

50 *Endymion*: a Carian shepherd with whom the moon-goddess, Selene, fell in love; either because she feared a rival or through the action of Zeus, Endymion fell into an unending sleep in a cave where Selene would visit him.

51 *Iasion*: an agricultural hero killed by Zeus for having slept with Demeter in a union which was later celebrated in mystery cults. Iasion himself was said to have founded the mysteries on Samothrace. The goatherd thus holds out to Amaryllis the prospect of secret knowledge gained by yielding to him.

IDYLL 4

An apparently inconsequential encounter between Battus and Corydon, who is looking after Aegon's cows while the latter is away at the Olympic Games. The poem, which is set in southern Italy, near Croton, at the western entrance to the Gulf of Tarentum, offers a vivid mimetic representation of the give-and-take of conversation.

2 *Aegon*: the name, which may have associations with the history of Croton where the poem is set, suggests 'Mr Goat'.

6 *Milon*: this character bears the name of a famous sixth-century wrestler from Croton who is credited with 31 victories at the great pan-Hellenic games.

6 *Alpheus*: the river at Olympia in the W. Peloponnese, site of the Olympic Games.

9 *Polydeuces*: one of the twin sons of Zeus, the Dioscuri, and invincible at boxing, cf. Idyll 22.

11 An obscure verse. Crazed wolves would do the same damage to the flock as this trip to Olympia, for which the sheep served as living 'supplies' for the notoriously large appetite of athletes, but it may also be relevant that the famous Milon (cf. n. above) was said to have been killed by wolves when he was caught in a tree which he was trying to tear apart.

16 *cicada*: that the diet of cicadas consisted entirely of dew is an idea found throughout antiquity, and one taken seriously by scientists as well as poets.

17 *Aesarus*: the modern Esaro, which flows into the sea at the site of Croton.

19 *Latymnus*: unknown; the scholiast claims that it is a mountain near Croton.

19 *Lampriadas*: it is unclear whether this is to be understood as the name of a local worthy or of the eponymous hero of the area.

21 *Hera*: cf. n. below, *the Lacinian shrine*.

24 *Neaethus*: a river north of Croton, perhaps the modern Neto.

29 *Pisa*: an old name for Olympia.

31 *Pyrrhus*: said by the scholiast to have been a lyric poet from Ionia or Lesbos, but otherwise unknown.

31 *Glauce*: a Chian musician, said to have been popular with Ptolemy Philadelphus; her songs were famously erotic.

32 *Croton*: once a great city, Croton had by this time suffered two centuries of warfare and was sacked during Rome's wars with Pyrrhus in the 270s.

32 *Zakynthos*: capital of the island of the same name in the Ionian Sea west of the Peloponnese. Corydon's song presumably began with a list of beautiful cities, none of which however could match Croton.

33 *the Lacinian shrine*: a great temple to Hera, the most important goddess of Magna Graecia, stood on the headland of Lacinion, SE of Croton; the headland is now Capo Colonna, from the one surviving column of the temple.

50 These verses seem to have some connection with a familiar sculptural motif of a boy taking a thorn from his foot or of one figure doing this service for another, cf. R. R. R. Smith, *Hellenistic Sculpture* (London, 1991), figs. 171–2.

IDYLL 5

A song-contest, conducted with real feeling, between a goatherd, Comatas, and a shepherd, Lacon, who are clearly old enemies. As with Idyll 4, the setting is south Italy.

2 *Sybaris*: a town in Magna Graecia, near Croton (cf. Idyll 4) on the

western side of the Gulf of Tarentum; it is, however, uncertain whether the name was still in general use at this time, or whether it had been completely replaced by the later settlement of Thurii (cf. 72). Theocritus may have associated it with a particular form of rustic song-contest.

16 *Crathis*: a river near Sybaris and Thurii.

20 *the pains of Daphnis*: cf. n. on p. 85.

23 *pig . . . Athena*: the proverb 'a pig and Athena' is more usually applied to those who 'teach their grandmothers to suck eggs' than to those who challenge their betters to a competition.

29 *wasps . . . cicadas*: cicadas are conventionally the most musically skilled of insects.

81 *Daphnis*: cf. n. on p. 85.

84 *Apollo . . . Carnean*: the Carnean festival was a major Dorian festival in honour of Apollo. Lacon tops Comatas' reference to the Muses with Apollo, the god of music, who is in charge of the Muses.

91 *apples*: cf. n. on p. 90.

105 *Praxiteles*: a famous Athenian sculptor of the fourth century BC. Comatas' hyperbole probably just means 'It's a wonderful piece of work!'.

121 *squills*: here used as a magical protection against Lacon's anger.

122 *Haleis*: unknown as a geographical feature near Sybaris; for the Coan Haleis cf. n. on p. 96.

123 *cyclamen*: a protection against evil to match Comatas' squills.

124 *Himera*: apparently here the name of a spring, but otherwise unknown.

133 *kissed by the ears*: a type of kiss in which one partner grasps the other's ears (like holding a pot) and kisses him/her.

138 *I order . . .*: Comatas' victory may be based on the fact that in v. 134 Lacon introduced a new character, Eumedes, thus contradicting his earlier love for Cratidas; this would explain why Comatas seems to claim victory in the immediately preceding couplet.

150 *Melanthius*: the goatherd of the *Odyssey* who was punished for his dealings with the suitors: 'they cut off his nose and ears with the ruthless bronze, tore out his parts to be eaten raw by dogs, and in savage fury lopped off his hands and feet' (22. 475–7, trans. W. Shewring).

IDYLL 6

This poem, like Idyll 11, centres around the love of the young Polyphemus, later to be the cannibal Cyclops of the *Odyssey*, for Galatea ('the lady of the milk'), a sea-nymph who may have been the object of cult on Sicily. The story of the young Polyphemus' passion for her was very popular in fourth-century poetry and drama, and Theocritus may have been particularly influenced by a dithyramb on this subject by Philoxenus of Cythera; the story is also often illustrated in the art of the Hellenistic and Roman periods. Whereas the Cyclops of Idyll 11 is hopelessly infatuated, Idyll 6 creates a more nuanced situation in which Polyphemus *may* for once have the controlling hand, though Galatea's existence, as described in Daphnis' song, remains as precarious and ephemeral as is appropriate for a sea-nymph: now you see her, now you don't.

1 *Aratus*: cf. the song of Simichidas in Idyll 7. This figure has sometimes been identified with the poet Aratus of Soli, whose astronomical poem, the *Phaenomena*, is still extant, but the case is not a strong one.

6 *apples*: cf. n. on p. 90, *Dionysus' apples*.

19 *moves her pieces*: a reference to a particular move in a board-game which was a sign of desperation or near-defeat.

23 *Telemus*: a prophet in the *Odyssey* who had predicted Polyphemus' blinding (*Odyssey* 9. 507–12).

38 *Parian marble*: the marble of Paros was famous for its purity and whiteness.

39 *the evil eye*: the danger here probably arises from Polyphemus' pride in his own (as he sees them) good looks. Spitting is frequently mentioned as a form of apotropaic magic, cf. 7. 127.

IDYLL 7

An account of an outing into the Coan countryside to attend a 'harvest festival'. The narrator, Simichidas, is depicted as an over-confident young poet, for whom 'bucolic' is simply one possible poetic code among many, whereas the mysterious Lycidas, who falls in with Simichidas and his friends on their way, seems genuinely to belong to and to understand the 'natural world'. The songs which the two poets exchange, two very different treatments of the theme of release from desire, seem also to offer two different visions of what bucolic song might be. The sudden appearance and amused smile of Lycidas suggest divinity, and his gift of a staff to the young Simichidas clearly recalls the investiture of Hesiod as a poet by the Muses in the opening of Hesiod's *Theogony*; if we are to understand that Lycidas is a god, then it is Apollo he most resembles (cf. below), but the pattern of (a mildly parodic) 'poetic initiation' is in any event clear. As for Simichidas, later antiquity took this as a pseudonym for Theocritus, but the relation between poet and narrating first-person will be rather more complex than that, and indeed the name, whatever its resonances which are now lost to us, is presumably chosen to prevent us making a simplistic assumption about the identity of the narrating voice.

The opening of the poem recalls the opening of a number of Plato's dialogues (*Lysis*, *Republic*), but its subject and manner bring it closest to the *Phaedrus*.

2　*Haleis*: a deme or village some ten kilometres west of Cos town.

3　*first-fruits*: a harvest offering to thank the goddess of crops, Demeter.

5　*Clytia and Chalcon*: grand names from local Coan history: Clytia ('Famous Lady') was the daughter of Merops, the original hero of the Coans, and Chalcon was her son.

7　*Burina*: probably modern Vourina, still an important water-source some 5 km south-west of Cos town.

10　*Brasilas*: presumably another figure of Coan legend; his 'tomb' has been attractively identified as Meso Vouno, a small hill about 4 km from Cos (W. G. Arnott, *Quaderni Urbinati*, 32 (1979), 99–105).

12　*Cydonia*: probably a Coan locality; the best known ancient Cydonia was, however, on the NW coast of Crete.

13　*Lycidas*: the name *may* evoke *lykios*, an epithet of Apollo.

40　*Sicelidas*: a name for Asclepiades of Samos, one of the greatest poets of the early Hellenistic period; only epigrams survive from his very varied output.

41　*Philitas*: a Coan, the greatest poet and scholar of the preceding generation, though only stray verses of his poetry survive; he acted as tutor to the young Ptolemy Philadelphus. It is very likely that Idyll 7 contains echoes of his work.

45　*stick*: a rustic equivalent of the staff which the Muses gave to

Hesiod when they instructed him in the art of poetry (*Theogony* 30–1).

46　*Mount Oromedon*: probably Mt. Dikeo, the highest ridge in the hills SW of Cos town; Oromedon seems to have had special associations with Apollo.

48　*singer who comes from Chios*: Homer.

52　*Mytilene*: the chief town of the island of Lesbos.

53　*the Kids . . . Orion*: both constellations are associated with stormy autumnal weather, but even so Ageanax will be safe, *if only he saves Lycidas . . .*

57　*halcyons*: the fourteen days around the winter solstice were, if calm, 'halcyon days', when these birds were believed to hatch their young.

60　*Nereids*: 'daughters of Nereus', sea nymphs.

65　*Ptelean wine*: the reference is unknown.

71　*Acharnae . . . Lycopa*: neither can be identified on Cos; the well-known Acharnae is a deme in Attica.

73　*Daphnis the cowherd*: cf. n. on p. 85.

75　*Himera*: river of central Sicily. We are probably to think of Stesichorus of the town of Himera, who wrote or was believed to have written a poem about Daphnis.

77　*Haemus . . . Caucasus*: Athos is the tallest mountain bordering the Aegean, Haemus and Rhodope are mountain ranges in what is now Bulgaria; for Greeks, the Caucasus formed the NE boundary of the known world.

79　*he will sing how once the goatherd . . .*: a South Italian folktale tells how a shepherd was kept alive with honeycombs by the Muses after he had been locked in a box by his angry master; whether or not the Comatas of 83 is to be identified with this goatherd is unclear.

93　*the throne of Zeus*: probably a hint at Ptolemy II Philadelphus, the ultimate patron for poets (cf. Idyll 17).

96　*The Loves sneezed*: a sneeze was always regarded by Greeks as an omen.

98　*Aratus*: cf. n. on p. 95.

99　*Aristis . . . best of men*: there is a pun on Aristis and *aristos*, Greek for 'best'.

100 *Phoebus*: Apollo, god of music.

103 *Homole*: an area in Thessaly; a particular association with Pan is not otherwise attested.

105 *Philinus*: cf. n. on p. 90.

107 This supposed Arcadian rite of beating (a statue of) the god in times of scarcity is otherwise unattested, though similar practices are known from many cultures. Arcadia, a backward and mountainous area of the Peloponnese, was particularly associated with Pan.

110 As the god of flocks and shepherds, Pan's punishment will consist of a radical reversal of the pastoral life: in midwinter he will herd in the frozen northern mountains and in the summer he will head for the burning southern plains.

111 *Edonian mountains*: the Edoni lived in the mountains between Macedonia and Thrace.

112 *River Hebrus*: the Hebrus (Maritsa) flows south from Bulgaria to the northern Aegean.

113 *Ethiopia*: i.e. Nubia and the northern Sudan.

114 *the Blemyan cliff*: the Blemyes were an 'Ethiopian' tribe.

116 *Byblis*: a spring at Miletus, as presumably was Hyetis.

116 *Oecus*: a Carian town near Miletus, associated with Aphrodite.

117 *Dione*: Aphrodite's mother, though perhaps here a name for Aphrodite herself.

127 *spit on us*: cf. n. on p. 95, *the evil eye*.

130 *Pyxa*: probably near modern Asphendiou. The name may have been particularly associated with Apollo.

148 *Castalia . . . Parnassus*: the spring and mountain of Delphi, Apollo's most important shrine.

149 *Chiron . . . Pholus*: the centaur Pholus entertained Heracles with some marvellous wine whose scent attracted the other centaurs; in the ensuing battle both Pholus and Chiron, the wisest of the centaurs and teacher of Achilles, were killed.

151 *Anapus*: a river at Syracuse. The reference is to the powerful wine with which Odysseus intoxicated the Cyclops Polyphemus so that he and his men could escape; Polyphemus subsequently hurled huge boulders at Odysseus' ship to try to prevent escape.

157 *the great winnowing-fan*: winnowing-fans were placed upright in heaps of grain to signal the end of the harvest.

158 *poppies and sheaves*: standard attributes of Demeter.

IDYLL 10

Idyll 10 stands out among the 'bucolic' poems because the characters are harvesters, not herdsmen, and there is a corresponding emphasis on agricultural labour, rather than herding, which is largely a matter of filling in the time. Milon opposes a 'Hesiodic' view of the necessity of unremitting labour to the sentimental fantasies of the lovesick Bucaeus. There is no indication of the poem's setting.

11 *dog tastes offal*: quasi-proverbial: once you start being in love, there is no end to it.

13 *wine from the cask . . .*: Milon sarcastically suggests that Bucaeus must be well off, with abundant supplies of food and drink, whereas he has to work all the time to scrape out a living.

14 *the field . . . is all unhoed*: it was common wisdom that being in love led to aimless daydreaming and put an end to work.

19 *Wealth*: poetry standardly represents the god Wealth as blind, cf. especially the *Plutus* ('Wealth') of Aristophanes.

24 *Pieria*: a mountainous region north of Mt. Olympus where the Muses were born.

28 *the printed orchid*: the *hyakinthos* is an unidentified mountain flower. Its dark pattern was thought to spell out AI, either the first two letters of Ajax's name, or the beginning of *aiai*, a cry of woe.

32 *Croesus*: a Lydian king of fabulous wealth, cf. Herodotus 1. 30–3.

39 *married his verse . . .*: Milon teases Bucaeus in the technical language of musical performance, but the exact meaning is uncertain.

41 *Lityerses*: a legendary Phrygian inventor of agriculture who was honoured in a reapers' song. Here 'manly' work-songs are ascribed to him.

55 *slicing cumin seeds*: 'cumin-splitting' was a proverbial expression for meanness.

57 *stringy love*: lovers were traditionally thin and wasted, and if Bucaeus does not work properly he will not eat.

IDYLL II

See the Introduction to Idyll 6. The principal ironies of this poem derive from our knowledge of the monstrous Cyclops of the *Odyssey* and of his fate; the lovesick wishes of the young Cyclops were to come only too true. The very idea of 'Polyphemus in love' derives its power from the solitary self-sufficiency of the Homeric figure, who was unmarried and a loner, even by Cyclopean standards.

This poem was famous in antiquity and is the primary model for Virgil's *Second Eclogue*.

1   *Nicias*: a doctor and poet from Miletus (cf. Idylls 13, 28). He wrote a poem, of which two verses survive, in response to Idyll II.

7   *my countryman*: the land of Homer's Cyclopes had long been identified with eastern Sicily.

10   *curls of hair*: this lovers' practice is not otherwise attested.

16   *Cypris*: Aphrodite ('lady of Cyprus').

26   *my mother*: the sea-nymph Thoosa.

53   *burn away . . . my single eye*: a pathetic foreshadowing of the Cyclops' ultimate fate at the hands of Odysseus.

60   *learn to swim*: Homer's Cyclopes had no ships, and Theocritus goes one better by making Polyphemus even unable to swim. 'Not knowing how to swim' was also a proverbial expression of ignorance.

61   *some mariner*: Odysseus, as it is to turn out.

75   *Milk the ewe at hand*: cf. Eng. 'a bird in the hand'.

80   *shepherded his love*: i.e. kept it under control.

81   *a large fee*: a teasing return to Nicias, the professional doctor.

IDYLL I2

An address by a man to the younger (male) object of his affections who, as the opening verses allow us to suspect, is not as faithful as the speaker would wish. The poem recalls the traditions of archaic paederastic poetry (Theognis, etc.), and its force lies in the contrast between the speaker's overheated wishes for happiness and our sense that it is all a delusion.

14 The speaker imagines himself and his beloved celebrated in song and with precious, and presumably ancient, dialect words for the usual *erastes* 'lover' and *eromenos* 'beloved'; this suits his self-deluding fantasies about the nature of his relationship with the young man. Amyclae was an ancient settlement near Sparta.

19 *Acheron*: the river which marked the boundary of the Underworld.

23 *pimples*: popular belief seems to have regarded pimples on the nose as a sign of telling lies.

27 *Nisaea*: the port of Megara on the Saronic gulf, W. of Athens.

29 The Megarians held annual games in honour of Diocles of Athens, though the connection between this hero and Megara is very obscure. There is no other evidence for a kissing-competition at his tomb.

35 *Ganymede*: the beautiful Trojan youth snatched up by Zeus to be his *eromenos* and wine-pourer.

36 *Lydian touchstone*: metals, such as gold, were tested by comparing the mark they made when rubbed against a 'touchstone' with the mark left by a piece of metal of known composition.

IDYLL 13

In a poem which bears strong formal similarities to Idyll 11, the poet tells Nicias (see n. on p. 100) the story of how Heracles lost his beloved squire Hylas, as an illustration of the fact that *eros* affects even heroes who later became immortal. Hylas seems originally to have been a figure from the local mythology of Mysia (NW Turkey); he was believed to have been snatched away by nymphs, and the inhabitants conducted regular ritual searches for him. He was later written into mythology as Heracles' squire, and the story of his loss to the Argonautic expedition became the explanation ('aetiology') for this ritual practice. Whether or not it was Apollonius (*Argonautica* 1. 1172–1357) and Theocritus who first created this combination we do not know.

2 The parentage of Eros was a notorious puzzle. The scholiast lists various possibilities taken from earlier poetry: Chaos and Earth, Ares and Aphrodite, Zephyros and Iris, etc.

5 *Amphitryon*: king of Thebes, and Heracles' mortal 'father', while Zeus was his immortal parent, cf. Idyll 24.

6   *the savage lion*: the Nemean lion, traditionally the object of Heracles' first labour.

16   *Jason . . . Golden Fleece*: the famous expedition of the Argonauts to the extreme eastern end of the Black Sea, cf. Pindar's *Pythian* 4, R. Hunter, *Apollonius of Rhodes, Jason and the Golden Fleece* (Oxford, 1995).

19   *Iolcus*: the Thessalian city (modern Volos) from which the Argonauts set out.

20   *Midea*: a town in the Argolid, where Alcmena's father, Electryon, was king.

22   *clashing rocks*: a legendary obstacle at the entrance to the Black Sea. By successfully passing between them, the Argonauts caused them to stand motionless forever after.

24   *Phasis*: the river of the kingdom of Colchis at the eastern edge of the Black Sea. The text here is very uncertain.

26   *the Pleiads' rising*: i.e. late April–early May, the start of the sailing season.

30   *Propontis*: the Sea of Marmara.

31   *Cianian people*: Cios is the modern Gemlik on the southern coast of the Sea of Marmara.

38   *Telamon*: a constant companion of Heracles in myth; he was Ajax's father and Achilles' uncle.

45   It is uncertain whether these names are traditional or a free invention by Theocritus. 'Malis' means apple-tree, and 'Nychea' is 'Lady of the night'.

49   *the Argive boy*: why Hylas is 'Argive' is uncertain. It has been suggested that the adjective actually refers to the gleaming white of his skin.

55   *the Scythian curve*: i.e. the type of bow in which two curved sections are joined by a straight 'waist' where the bow is held.

58   The repeated 'three times' points to an explanation for the Mysian ritual practice, and the verses also suggest a version in which, after his disappearance, Hylas was metamorphosed into Echo.

75   Theocritus follows a version in which Heracles did finally reach Colchis, though in Apollonius he is lost to the expedition forever.

inhospitable: the Black Sea was originally called *Axeinos*, 'inhospit-
able', as it was to prove for the Argonauts; the more familiar
Euxeinos, 'hospitable', is a euphemism.

IDYLL 14

The setting for this mime-like conversation, which shows an important
debt to the traditions of comedy, is not made explicit. The final eulogy of
Ptolemy Philadelphus, however, associates it with Idylls 15 and 17 (cf.
above, p. ix). The motif of foreign military service as a response to a
broken heart is familiar in New Comedy.

5   *a Pythagorist*: a contemptuous reference to an adherent to the
ascetic precepts of Pythagoras (late 6th cent. BC); those claiming to
follow him are often mocked in comedy as dirty and hypocritical
in their allegiance to 'the simple life'.

6   Athens was still the centre of Greek philosophical life; Thyonichus
may hint that the claim of Athenian origin was one more decep-
tion practised by this rogue.

13   *trainer*: lit. 'horse-pursuer'; the exact sense is uncertain.

15   *Bibline wine*: a very old name for a prized wine, but the reference,
whether to a place or a grape or vine-variety, is uncertain;
Aeschinas may mean little more than 'very fine wine'.

18   *onion*: *bolbos* is in fact a kind of bulbous hyacinth, believed, like
snails, to have aphrodisiac powers.

19   *toast his loved one in neat wine*: cf. n. on p. 90, *unmixed wine*.

24   *'Seen a wolf?'*: there was a popular belief that if a wolf saw someone
before itself being seen, that person was struck dumb.

30   *Larisa*: a town in central Thessaly. Unfortunately, nothing is
known of the 'wolf' song here referred to.

43   *the bull once fled to the wood*: proverbial for someone who has dis-
appeared without a trace.

46   *a Thracian haircut*: obviously unflattering (to Thracians), but the
exact sense is unknown.

49   *the poor Megarians*: a reference to a story that the Megarians, on
asking the Delphic oracle whether any city was better than theirs,
were told that they were 'neither third, nor fourth nor twelfth, and
did not even enter into the calculation'.

51   *the mouse . . . tasting pitch*: 'a mouse tastes pitch' was used proverbially of someone whose troubles are only just beginning; presumably the mouse falls into the pitch-barrel and perishes.

61   *a lover of arts and women*: for Ptolemy's patronage of the arts cf. above, p. ix; he married (at least) twice, and history records a string of mistresses after the death of his second wife, Arsinoe.

66   *on your right shoulder*: obviously a distinctive sign of military dress.

67   The type of fighting envisaged is that of the hoplite phalanx.

IDYLL 15

Two Syracusan women resident in Alexandria go to the royal palace to witness a festival of Adonis which Queen Arsinoe is staging in honour of her mother Berenice. As quintessential figures of the mime (a genre here signalled by the change of setting within the poem), the women at some level represent the arrival of the Syracusan mime-poet, namely Theocritus, at the court of Philadelphus. Festivals of Adonis (1. 109 n.) were held annually to celebrate the young god's return from the Underworld, and the focus of the poem is the contrast between the low aspirations and straitened circumstances of the women and the luxury and display of the palace. The 'hymn to Adonis' with which the poem ends mixes features of 'real' hymns with description in a way which is characteristic of poetic representations of festival practice, such as Callimachus' *Hymns* to Athena and Demeter.

32   *enough for the gods*: i.e. as far as the gods allow me.

40   '*Nasty witch*': Praxinoa threatens the child with 'Mormo', a familiar Greek 'bogey-man'.

46   *your father went immortal*: Philadelphus instituted an Alexandrian cult in honour of his father, Ptolemy I Soter, cf. Idyll 17; Soter's wife, Berenice, was subsequently added to this cult of the *Theoi Soteres*, the 'Saviour Gods'.

48   A low regard for their moral character was one Greek view of the Egyptians.

63   *The Greeks entered Troy by trying*: it took them, however, ten years to do so.

66   *how Zeus married Hera*: a subject which was in fact known only to these two immortals (cf. *Iliad* 14. 295–6). There may be a reference to Ptolemy and Arsinoe (cf. Idyll 17).

77 *'All the women inside'*: entirely obscure, nor is it known whether Praxinoa's explanation, 'as the man said when . . .', has any genuine connection with the semi-proverbial saying.

80 *Athena*: patron goddess of crafts such as weaving.

86 *Acheron*: cf. n. on p. 101.

88 The stranger finds the 'broad' Doric vowels of Praxinoa and Gorgo grating. His words are themselves Doric, but we are perhaps to imagine that Syracusan was felt to be particularly broad.

91 *Corinth*: Syracuse was originally a Corinthian colony. Bellerophon was a mythical Corinthian prince whose story is told at *Iliad* 6. 152–202. A life of exile and quest began when he was falsely accused of attempted rape by the queen of Tiryns (cf. 'Potiphar's wife'); legend also associates him with the winged horse Pegasus.

92 *Peloponnesian*: i.e. 'pure and original' Doric, as Praxinoa perceives it.

93 *Persephone*: queen of the Underworld; women often invoked her in oaths.

93 *except one, that is*: Ptolemy Philadelphus, of course.

100 *Golgi*: the site (not certainly identified) of a cult of Aphrodite on Cyprus.

100 *Eryx*: a high mountain in the far west of Sicily, sacred to Aphrodite.

100 *Idalium*: modern Dali in central Cyprus, another site of Aphrodite's worship.

102 *the Hours*: cf. n. on p. 87. Here they are associated with the return of spring and fruitfulness.

105 *Cypris*: cf. n. on p. 87.

105 *Berenice*: the mother of Philadelphus and Arsinoe.

110 *Helen*: Ptolemaic poets made extensive use of the paradigmatic virtues of Helen, despite her rather chequered career in legend. According to one version, she had in fact 'sat out' the Trojan War in Egypt (cf. Euripides' *Helen*), and she was the object of cult there.

123 *a boy to pour his wine*: Ganymede, cf. n. on p. 101.

124 Miletus was famous throughout antiquity for wool, though Samos is not elsewhere cited in this context.

135 The women's lamentation, the most famous part of the rituals for Adonis, will mark the annual return of Adonis to the Underworld after his period on earth.

137 Many in this catalogue are not 'demigods' in the strict sense, but the word is used more generally of the great figures of the heroic age (cf. Idyll 17).

137 *Agamemnon*: leader of the Greek expedition to Troy.

138 *Ajax*: one of the greatest Greek heroes at Troy; he killed himself in anger at not being awarded Achilles' arms after the latter's death.

138 *Hector*: the greatest Trojan hero of the war.

139 *Patroclus*: the doomed companion of Achilles.

139 *Pyrrhus*: Achilles' son, also called Neoptolemus, who subsequently became an object of cult at Delphi.

141 *Lapiths*: a race of heroes earlier in time than the Trojan War; their battle with the centaurs is often depicted in Greek art.

141 *Deucalion*: the Greek 'Noah', who survived the flood and refounded the human race.

142 *Pelops*: the eponymous hero of the Peloponnese, whose family included the house of Agamemnon.

143 *Pelasgian kings of Argos*: the Pelasgians were believed to be the pre-Greek inhabitants of Greece, and poetry often associates them with Argos, though this may be based on a misunderstanding. Homer mentions a 'Pelasgian Argos' in Thessaly (*Iliad* 2. 681).

IDYLL 16

A poem in honour of Hieron II, who became tyrant of Syracuse *c.*275 BC. In the fifth century Hieron I had been a famous patron of poets such as Pindar, and Theocritus aims to recreate that relationship with his namesake. The poem is indeed full of echoes of the great lyric poetry in honour of patrons by Pindar and Simonides, but its tone and direction are determined by a clear sense that times have changed and that the past cannot be recreated.

6 *my Graces*: the Graces had a traditional role in conferring 'grace' upon poets and their poems, and here Theocritus goes one step further and personifies his poems as 'Graces'. He then imagines

them as a band of children who go from house to house seeking a favourable reception, i.e. patronage; cf. modern 'trick or treating'. In v. 10 ('empty box') they are once again a set of papyrus rolls.

31   *Acheron*: see n. on p. 101.

35   These verses refer to various Thessalian patrons of the great poet Simonides of Ceos (late sixth–early fifth century).

39   *plain of Crannon*: a town in central Thessaly.

46   *their swift horses*: Simonides was famous, like Pindar, for 'epinician' poems in honour of victories at the great athletic festivals.

48   *champions of Lycia*: such as Glaucus and Sarpedon in the *Iliad*.

49   *Cycnus*: a son of Poseidon who was killed by Achilles at Troy; his story figures in the epic cycle. His name means 'swan', and was said to derive from the whiteness of his skin, hence 'womanish', or from his hair.

54   Eumaeus and Philoetius looked after, respectively, the pigs and the cattle on Odysseus' estate on Ithaca.

55   *Laertes*: Odysseus' father.

56   *an Ionian*: many cities claimed Homer, but tradition and the language of the poems particularly associated him with Asia Minor and the Ionian islands near its coast. In Idylls 7 and 22 Theocritus uses the tradition that he came from Chios.

75   *Simois*: the river at Troy.

75   *the tomb of Phrygian Ilus*: a landmark at Troy in the *Iliad*.

76   *the Phoenicians*: i.e. the Carthaginians, who by tradition had come from Phoenicia to settle in North Africa. Theocritus refers to a planned attack upon them by Hieron II of Syracuse.

77   *Libya*: this name may be given to any part of North Africa west of the Nile.

83   Persephone ('the Maiden') and her mother Demeter were particular protectors of Syracuse. Ephyra is an old name for Corinth, from where Syracuse was originally settled.

84   *Lysimeleia*: a lake at Syracuse.

99   *the Scythian sea*: Scythia is here used to mark the NE boundary of the known world.

100   *pitch-packed battlements*: i.e. Babylon, whose brick walls, held

together by bitumen, were one of the wonders of the ancient world; Babylon, together with Scythia, here defines the eastern edge of the world. Semiramis was a queen of Babylon around whom many fabulous legends grew up.

102 *Arethusa*: the famous spring of Syracuse.

104 *Eteocles*: a legendary king of Orchomenus in Boeotia (NW of Athens) who is said to have founded the famous cult of the Graces there.

105 *Minyan Orchomenus*: The Minyai were believed to have been the early inhabitants of various areas of central Greece.

IDYLL 17

An encomium of Ptolemy II Philadelphus ('sister-loving'), who reigned from 282 to his death in 246, and his sister and wife Arsinoe whom he married at some time in the middle of the 270s. The poem celebrates the links of the royal house with Alexander and Heracles, and is our only surviving example of what seems to have been a very common type of poem in the Hellenistic period.

9 *Ida*: the wooded mountain near Troy.

13 Philadelphus' father was Ptolemy I Soter ('the Saviour'), son of a Macedonian noble called Lagus.

15 *The Father*: i.e. Zeus.

22 The Ptolemies, like Alexander and the Macedonian royal house before them, claimed descent from Heracles.

33 *Berenice*: daughter of Antigone, wife of Ptolemy I and mother of Philadelphus and his sister-wife Arsinoe.

34 *Dione*: mother of Aphrodite.

46 *Acheron*: cf. n. on p. 101.

50 There is little other evidence for the deification of Berenice, but it was a common practice for one deity to be given a 'share' in the temple of another.

53 *lady of Argos*: Deipyle, an Argive princess.

53 *Calydon*: an Aetolian town above the western end of the Gulf of Corinth.

54 *Diomedes*: one of the fiercest Greek fighters at Troy.

58 Philadelphus was born on Cos in 308. Theocritus, like Callimachus in his *Hymn to Delos*, suggests an analogy between the birth of Ptolemy and that of Apollo on Delos as described in the *Homeric Hymn to Apollo*.

65 *hill of Triopia*: Cape Crio, on the Turkish mainland SE of Cos, and site of Cnidus and a temple of 'Triopian Apollo', where an important Doric festival was held.

69 *Rhenaea*: a small island near Delos, dedicated to Apollo.

84 For these areas of Ptolemaic influence see the map. p. xxiv.

111 *Dionysus' sacred contest*: Dramatic and poetic festivals flourished at Alexandria; we hear of a group of tragic poets called 'the Pleiad'.

115 *sons of Atreus*: Agamemnon and Menelaus.

123 Philadelphus established the cult of his parents as the 'Saviour Gods'.

134 *Iris*: the messenger of the gods, who here apparently has the role of bedroom attendant for Zeus and Hera.

IDYLL 18

A recreation of an archaic Spartan wedding-song, such as is familiar to us from the poetry of Alcman; the scholia also tell us that Theocritus has borrowed from the *Helen* of Stesichorus (early sixth century), a narrative poem which seems to have dealt in some detail with Helen's early years. Spartan antiquities were of considerable interest in the third century, and such a poetic reconstruction is a very good example of the recuperative focus of much Hellenistic poetry. It has been attractively suggested that this poem, like Idylls 15 and 17, should be set within the context of the Ptolemaic stress on marital devotion and happiness; Helen enjoyed cult status in Egypt, and the early Ptolemies and their poets seem to have refashioned her into a model of womanly virtue.

9 Teasing the bridegroom is a standard element of wedding-songs.

12 *her doting mother*: Leda.

15 *a good man's sneeze*: sneezes were always considered as omens, for good or ill.

19 *daughter of Zeus*: like Heracles, Helen had two 'fathers', Zeus and her mother's husband Tyndareus.

23 *Eurotas*: a river at Sparta.

24 *oiling ourselves like men*: the athletic pursuits of Spartan maidens were a familiar element of the standard image of Sparta in the ancient world; cf. v. 39.

43 No more is known of this tree-cult of Helen at Sparta, but Theocritus presumably refers to a real or believed cult practice connected with weddings. The interest in the origins of cult ('aetiology') is typical of Hellenistic poetry.

50 Leto was the mother of Apollo and Artemis, and hence here a paradigm of a mother with glorious children.

51 *Cypris*: Aphrodite, the 'lady of Cyprus'.

58 *Hymen Hymenaeus*: a version of the ritual cry or refrain which accompanied weddings. Hymen or Hymenaeus is sometimes personified as a son of Aphrodite.

IDYLL 22

A hymn to the Dioscuri which, while traditional in form, innovates in hymning each twin separately and in the clear experimentation with mood and tone produced by the contrast between the two narratives. As with Helen in Idyll 18, the Dioscuri may have been particularly associated with the Ptolemaic house.

5 *Thestius' child*: Leda.

6 Two of the most familiar attributes of the Dioscuri were their horsemanship ('horse-taming' is a stock epithet of Castor in early epic, cf. 33) and their saving interventions from shipwreck.

21 In his poem on the constellations and weather signs, Aratus notes that the sudden disappearance of the Manger, a star cluster in the middle of Cancer, marks the coming of a bad storm (*Phaenomena* 892–908); here its return signals clearing weather. The 'Asses' are two faint stars on either side of 'the Manger'.

26 The story of Polydeuces' boxing-match with Amycus is also told by Apollonius in the *Argonautica* (2. 1–163); as with the story of Hylas (Idyll 13), it is clear that the two poetic versions are not independent.

29 *Bebryces*: Theocritus places this people on the south-west coast of the Black Sea, whereas Apollonius puts the encounter within the Propontis before the Clashing Rocks. See the map.

52 This exchange of conversation ('stichomythia') in hexameters is virtually unparalleled in Greek poetry.

79 *Thessalian ship*: the Argo was launched from Pagasae, the port of Iolcus (near modern Volos) at the head of the Magnesian Gulf in Thessaly.

87 *son of Tyndareus*: for this double parentage cf. n. on p. 109, *daughter of Zeus*.

92 *Tityos-like monster*: the huge Tityos tried to rape Leto and was confined and tortured for his crime in Tartarus; cf. *Odyssey* 11. 576–81.

122 *Amyclae*: a small town near Sparta with which the Dioscuri were often associated.

138 *the daughters of Leucippus*: Theocritus combines the abduction by the Dioscuri of these girls with the traditional story (the cyclic *Cypria*; Pindar, *Nemean* 10) of a dispute between the Dioscuri and Idas and Lynceus, the sons of Aphareus; whether or not Theocritus had literary sources for this combination is unclear.

154 Elis, Arcadia, and Achaea are all regions of the Peloponnese. Sisyphus was a legendary king of Corinth.

170 It is disputed whether there is now a lacuna in which Castor started to reply or whether Lynceus' speech continues (in which case 'brother' in 172 will be 'blood relation' and we must read 'Castor' for 'Lynceus' in 176).

217 *singer of Chios*: Homer.

IDYLL 24

A narrative poem telling the story of the infant Heracles' strangling of the snakes which the jealous Hera sent to destroy him, and of his upbringing. The end of the poem is lost, but there is some indication that it contained a prayer by the poet to the now divine Heracles for victory in a poetic contest. The concentration on domestic detail and the amusing account of Amphitryon in bed well illustrate how Hellenistic poetry took an innovative attitude to traditional 'heroic' material. Among Theocritus' important sources for Heracles' killing of the snakes are two Pindaric versions of these events, *Nemean* 1 and *Paean* 20.

1 *Midea*: a town in the Argolis, where Alcmena's father Electryon was king.

2 *Iphicles*: in the traditional story Heracles was the child of Zeus and Alcmena, and his 'twin' Iphicles the child of Alcmena and her husband Amphitryon, cf. the *Amphitruo* of Plautus.

4 A late source records that Ptolemy I had been exposed by his father in a shield.

5 *Pterelaus*: a Taphian king who had been betrayed by his daughter to the invading Amphitryon; it was while he was away on this expedition that Zeus fooled Alcmena into sleeping with him.

47 This mill-slave is taken from *Odyssey* 20. 105–6.

64 *Teiresias*: the blind Theban prophet, most familiar to us from the story of Oedipus.

83 *Trachis*: a town in central Greece near Thermopylae.

84 *a son of the gods*: Heracles married Hebe, the daughter of Zeus and Hera.

96 *without a backward glance*: a very common element in magical and ritual instructions.

105 *Linus*: more usually a legendary figure comparable to Orpheus, he is said to have taught Heracles music, though he is also connected with the invention of Greek script.

106 *Eurytus*: from Oechalia; he is mentioned in the *Odyssey* (8. 224), together with Heracles, as a great archer of the previous generation.

110 *Eumolpus*: the name 'fair-singing' is very appropriate, although this character is otherwise quite obscure; Philammon, however, was a son of Apollo and a musician.

115 *Harpalycus of Panopeus*: otherwise unknown; Panopeus is a town in Phocis. Another source names 'Autolycus' (perhaps Odysseus' grandfather, also connected with Hermes) as Heracles' teacher in wrestling.

127 *Castor, Hippalus' son*: otherwise unknown.

130 Tydeus was exiled from Calydon in Aetolia and married the daughter of Adrastus, king of Argos; their son was Diomedes.

IDYLL 26

A hymn to Dionysus retelling the grisly story, most familiar from Euripides' *Bacchae* (of which there are many echoes in this poem), of how Dionysus punished the Theban women for refusing to accept that he was the son of Zeus by sending them into a Dionysiac frenzy, in the course of which Agave led the murder of her son Pentheus who had come to spy on the women's rites. This frustratingly mysterious poem is perhaps to be associated with the many groups of Dionysiac initiates which flourished in the Hellenistic period.

4   *Semele*: a Theban princess and mother of Dionysus, who was burnt up by Zeus' fire when she persuaded him to appear to her in his full brilliance.

25 *not Pentheus but mourning*: the Greek has an untranslatable pun, as *penthos* is Greek for 'grief'.

26 These tantalizing verses have yet to yield up their secrets; they would seem to be connected with the Dionysiac cults and associations which flourished in the Hellenistic age. It deepens the mystery that 26–7 ('What *I* pray for . . . who are pure') are very like a verse of Callimachus which is also connected with Thebes (*Hymn to Delos* 97).

33 *Dracanus*: a traditional birth-site of Dionysus (cf. *Homeric Hymn to Dionysus* 1), but whether Theocritus thought of this as an island or a mountain, and where he placed it, is unknown.

34 After saving the unborn Dionysus from Semele's womb, Zeus hid the baby from Hera's wrath in his thigh.

35 *Cadmus' city*: Cadmus was the legendary founder of Thebes.

IDYLL 28

In metre and language this poem recreates the archaic Lesbian lyric of Sappho and Alcaeus. While presenting his wife with a distaff, Theocritus presents his friend Nicias, who was himself a poet, with a choice poetic virtuosity.

2 *Neileus*: the legendary founder of Miletus.

4 *Cypris*: i.e. Aphrodite, the lady of Cyprus.

5 *Nicias*: cf. n. on p. 100.

13 *Theugenis*: Nicias' wife.

17 *Archias*: the legendary Corinthian founder of Syracuse; Ephyra was an old name for Corinth.

IDYLL 29

Another recreation of archaic Lesbian lyric and the paederastic themes of the great sympotic poetry of the past; the speaker's voice is not unlike that of the deluded speaker of Idyll 12.

1 *in vino veritas*: the Greek is a semi-proverbial tag, which Theocritus quotes in a version from the opening of a poem by the archaic Lesbian poet Alcaeus, 'wine, dear lad, and truth'.

34 *Achilles . . . Patroclus*: assumed in post-Homeric tradition (at least) to have been lovers, faithful even after death.

37 *the golden apples*: Heracles fetched the Golden Apples of the Hesperides from the far west of the world as one of his labours.

37 *Cerberus*: the terrible watchdog of the Underworld, who was brought to earth by Heracles as another of his labours.

IDYLL 30

Another paederast's monologue, in the language and metre of archaic Lesbian lyric.

American Literature

British and Irish Literature

Children's Literature

Classics and Ancient Literature

Colonial Literature

Eastern Literature

European Literature

History

Medieval Literature

Oxford English Drama

Poetry

Philosophy

Politics

Religion

The Oxford Shakespeare

A complete list of Oxford Paperbacks, including Oxford World's Classics, Oxford Shakespeare, Oxford Drama, and Oxford Paperback Reference, is available in the UK from the Academic Division Publicity Department, Oxford University Press, Great Clarendon Street, Oxford OX2 6DP.

In the USA, complete lists are available from the Paperbacks Marketing Manager, Oxford University Press, 198 Madison Avenue, New York, NY 10016.

Oxford Paperbacks are available from all good bookshops. In case of difficulty, customers in the UK can order direct from Oxford University Press Bookshop, Freepost, 116 High Street, Oxford OX1 4BR, enclosing full payment. Please add 10 per cent of published price for postage and packing.